The Other Side
of
Delinquency

Waln K. Brown

A Volume in the
Crime, Law,
and Deviance Series

The Other Side
of
Delinquency

Waln K. Brown

Rutgers University Press
New Brunswick, NJ

Library of Congress Cataloging in Publication Data
Brown, Waln K., 1944–
The other side of delinquency.

(Crime, law, and deviance)
Includes index.
1. Brown, Waln K., 1944–.
2. Juvenile delinquents—
United States—Biography.
I. Title.   II. Series.

HV9104.B77   1983   364.3'6'0924 [B]   82–23162
ISBN 0-8135-0993-9
ISBN 0-8135-0994-7 (pbk.)

To the memory
of my mother,
whose pain
was far greater.

I could never have achieved what I have done had I been stubbornly set on clinging to my origins, to the remembrances of my youth. In fact, to give up being stubborn was the supreme commandment I laid upon myself; free ape as I was, I submitted myself to that yoke. In revenge, however, my memory of the past has closed the door against me more and more. I could have returned at first, had human beings allowed it, through an archway as wide as the span of heaven over the earth, but as I spurred myself on in my forced career, the opening narrowed and shrank behind me; I felt more comfortable in the world of men and fitted it better; the strong wind that blew after me out of my past began to slacken; today it is only a gentle puff of air that plays around my heels; and the opening in the distance, through which it comes and through which I once came myself, has grown so small that, even if my strength and my will power sufficed to get me back to it, I should have to scrape the very skin from my body to crawl through. To put it plainly, much as I like expressing myself in images, to put it plainly: your life as apes, gentlemen, insofar as something of that kind lies behind you, cannot be farther removed from you than mine is from me.

Franz Kafka
A Report to an Academy

Contents

Foreword   xi

Acknowledgments   xiii

1
The White Room   1

2
A House Is Not a Home   9

3
School Days   19

4
A Day in Court   26

5
Street Life   39

6
A Probation Officer's Point of View   45

7
The State Hospital   65

8
In a Corner   71

9
Psychiatric Assessment   76

10
A Return to Sickness   86

11
Official Viewpoints   91

12
Welcome to Reform School   105

13
Initial Adjustments   112

14
The Social Order   119

15
Hit Men and Heroes   125

16
Spare the Rod and Spoil the Child   136

17
Of Time and Temperament   142

18
Through Official Eyes   152

19
A Period of Adjustment   168

20
The Other Side of Delinquency   180

Foreword

For a professional man to expose the intimate particulars of his disrupted family origins and his youthful delinquency requires great courage. Waln Brown has undertaken this task in the hope of throwing light on the little understood process whereby many one-time delinquents mature into solid citizens. His subsequent adult experience as an observer of the juvenile justice system, combined with his early experiences as a client of that system, provided an unusual opportunity for insightful comment. An additional advantage is his remarkable facility for distancing himself from traumatic experiences of the past, recollecting them without bitterness, and recognising the good as well as the bad aspects of the behaviour of parents and social agencies, even though at the time they must often have seemed unredeemably hostile.

The product is a valuable case study, but like all single case studies it has to be viewed as a unique story the elements of which may or may not be widely generalisable. In one respect, however, it is indisputably typical, namely that no single factor or event can be pin-pointed as the overriding reason for the successful outcome. It is evident that the young Waln, unlike the majority of persistent delinquents, had the advantage of a sound intelligence and the capacity to absorb scholastic knowledge once the emotional blockages were overcome. He was also fortunate in developing a physique which helped him to hold his own and acquire status in an institutional environment that rewarded aggressive self-assertion.

Reading this account one cannot but remark upon the insensitivity, verging upon cruelty, of some of the regimes in residential institutions for delinquents. The description of a psychiatric assessment in a large state hospital is little short of horrific. The conflict between recognition of an unsuitable home environment and awareness of the disadvantages of institutional placement is one of the great difficulties faced by practitioners. Waln Brown's account also highlights the relative powerlessness of social work and educational interventions in the face of a malignant home environment.

Sociologists may be critical of this work because it does not attempt to deal in any direct way with the socio-economic and class-cultural forces that shape lives and largely determine the incidence of such phenomena as the generation gap, alienation from school, broken homes, and material deprivation. On the other hand, it does call attention to an aspect unfairly neglected in present day criminological thinking, that is the qualities of the individual "deviant" and the quality of the persons who interact with him, whether as relatives or professional helpers. These are as important as external social circumstances in determining the chances of the rebellious young delinquent becoming a confirmed outcast and criminal or settling down to a more disciplined socially acceptable life-style.

A unique feature of this book is the use of documentary records, old case notes and assessments, setting out the official views of the authorities, which sometimes contrast sadly with the recollections of how it seemed at the time to the boy himself. This highlights the essentially subjective nature of many professional judgements about delinquents and the frequent failure to comprehend the situation from the juvenile's standpoint. It also illustrates the tendency to try to make dubious interpretations of behaviour seem more convincing by dressing them up in high sounding jargon. If this aspect is taken to heart by readers who are themselves engaged in such work the book should perform a valuable service.

D. J. West, M.D.
Director
Institute of Criminology
University of Cambridge

Acknowledgments

The process of writing this book bears great similarity to the living of my life. There were many obstacles to overcome as I struggled to translate the painful experiences of my early years into something meaningful. The self-imposed reliving of those long repressed events took me through many changes. I endured periods of anger, anxiety, confusion, depression, doubt; but it was a necessary catharsis that brought me closer to a clearer understanding of myself and others. Each succeeding draft served to purge the long-standing emotional conflicts working on my actions and perceptions. Little by little I grew more in touch with the reality of what had happened, less encumbered by defense mechanisms that had outlived their usefulness.

Yet what I have managed to accomplish was not done alone. As in any life, delinquent or otherwise, many people played an integral role in the eventual outcome. The writing of this book has brought that point home. Throughout my life the people who have offered support, guidance, love, and understanding have been the critical difference between what I am and what I might have been. Such is also the case with this book. During the nearly six years I wrestled with the ensuing pages, there were numerous times when I felt defeated or otherwise unable to continue. Fortunately, there was always someone to pick me up, dust me off, and redirect me toward my goal. It is to these otherwise anonymous sources of inspiration that this section speaks in an attempt to express the deep appreciation I have for their individual suggestions, help, and friendship. Though I must take full responsibility for the contents of this book, these people had much to do with supplying the context in which it was completed: E. James Anthony, Lee and Pat Brown, Emmanuel Cassamatis, Charlotte Garman, William and Ruth Gladden, Bob Graham, L. C. Heim, Cynthia Hill, E. Hunter Hurst, Carolyn Kohr, Bill Mader, Cheryl and J. D. Mercier, T. P. Miller, Delores and Thom Neptune, Ron Sharp, Dan Smith, Jay Smith, and D. J. West. A special thanks to Stuart Mitchner for his editorial improvements. But, most of all, thanks to Christine A. Leber, friend and lover, who stood with me through this ordeal.

I should also note that as a matter of personal and legal discretion the names of individuals other than my family, William Gladden, Kenneth Goldstein, and E. Hunter Hurst have been changed throughout to protect their privacy.

Waln K. Brown, Director
The William Gladden Foundation

The Other Side
of
Delinquency

1

The White Room

June 8, 1960, life hit rock bottom. The decline had already begun, but it was not until that day between my fifteenth and sixteenth birthdays that my loose grip on life finally gave way.

Though twenty-one years have passed since then, I remember that day as if it had just happened. It was like most days that announce the coming of summer: a soft blue sky, robin red-breasts poking their beaks into the freshly mown green grass, the scent of flowers floating on a gentle breeze, the sun spreading its warmth everywhere. School would be over in two days. Summer vacation was almost at hand. It should have been a time for celebration. Yet there was no happiness within me, only confusion and a sense of impending doom.

What was happening inside me could be seen on the surface. Dandruff flaked from an oily scalp. One part or another of my body was in constant nervous motion. But, worst of all, from forehead to chest, I was infected by a mass of pimples, boils, and open sores. For years I had been a continued source of income for the medical profession. Dermatologists had prescribed a variety of antibiotics, ointments, soaps, and ultraviolet treatments designed to combat symptoms. Psychologists and psychiatrists had plumbed my brain in an attempt to understand the causes of my problems. All efforts had fallen woefully short.

1

One week before that June day, I had begun taking a new "wonder drug" for the acne. It did nothing to stop the pimples; instead, I became tired and weak. I experienced the sensation of floating. It was as if I were on a hallucinogenic "trip" where body and mind were at odds. One moment I could barely lift my head; a moment later I could not remain still.

Then it happened. Something inside me gave way and I ran from the house screaming that I would cut my face with a razor, that I hoped a car would hit me. I wanted to die. I ran, and ran, and ran until my lungs almost burst; when dizziness and exhaustion overtook me, I hid in a field. But with the approach of night, I forced myself home and curled up on the back porch to sleep. There was nowhere else to go.

Mother found me that night, huddled in a corner. A short time later, three township policemen came to the house, carried me to their car, then deposited me at the county hospital. I was too weak to resist. Sleep was my only escape.

When I awoke mother was standing over me, pressing my limp hand, trying to soothe me back to life.

"Waln. Waln. Can you hear me, darling?"

"Where am I?"

"You're in the hospital. Don't you remember?"

"Oh. Yeah. But why did you have them bring me here?"

"Because I was afraid something was wrong with you. That's the reason I had the policemen bring you here. I just wanted to be sure you were safe and well. I only wanted to help you."

"Help! The only way you can help me is by leaving me alone!"

"But Waln, I love you."

"You don't love me! You never did! You're just like him! You want me out of your life, too! Well, I don't care anymore! Get away from me! I don't love you, either!"

I grabbed the plastic pitcher from atop the nightstand and hurled it across the room. It bounced off the wall onto the floor. A patient screamed. A nurse rushed into the room and crossed toward me. I kicked out, knocking her off balance. Another scream. Suddenly the room was filled with people wearing white uniforms. I kicked and punched. A man vised my wrists. Another man sank a needle deep into the flesh. The room began to whirl.

The hospital records indicate that sodium amytol had been the drug used to stop my outburst. The records further disclose that since my admission to the hospital I had also been given dosages of Nembutal, Tofranil, Spraine and tetracycline hydrochloride. Perhaps the presence of these medications in my system helps to account, in part, for what followed.

When I revived from the drugged sleep, I was in a stupor. Only the sound of distant voices indicated I was still alive. I tried to gather myself together. I scanned the room. This was not the ward where I had first been put. But, then, where?

I was in a small white room. The cot I was sprawled on was metal. The off-white surface was severely chipped and scratched. A faint smell of urine rose from the thin mattress beneath the heavily starched sheets. Somewhere below, wire springs squeaked with the slightest movement.

To the right, beside the cot, was a metal nightstand, its surface as battered as the cot's. On the stand were a plastic pitcher, a paper cup, and a box of tissues.

The left wall held a large window. There was no slack in the thin wire mesh that filled it. Beyond the wire window was another, much larger, window made of milky glass. A thin corridor ran between them.

On the right wall was a door that looked to be made of thick, heavy metal—like a vault. Near its top was a small wire-filled window.

The far wall was blank. Only the pale gray floor broke the monotony of the off-white color that suffocated the room.

Above, beyond reach, a lone bare bulb was screwed into the ceiling. It was the sun of the small white room.

It seemed like hours before I could gather the strength to move. All the while, the same questions throbbed through my brain: Where was I? Why had I been put there? When would I get out?

Finally, with great effort, I rolled off the cot onto the gray tile floor, crawled to the wall, and inched to a shaky stance. Weak-kneed, I eased myself toward the door and peeked with bleary eyes through the small wire window into the hallway. Nobody was there. Only the occasional sound of muffled voices disturbed the quiet.

I tested the door with the weight of my body. It did not budge. A shoulder thrown at the stubborn door produced only a mocking thud. The voices stopped. I pressed tightly against the wall, holding my breath. The voices began again. Stale air exploded from my aching lungs.

The large, screened window caught my eye. No light found its way through the thick milky pane beyond the screening. Scanning the screen in search of escape, I stumbled toward it and checked the tension of the mesh. Each thin wire was anchored deep within the metal frame. I pressed my palms against the woven obstacle and pushed. Nothing. I put all my remaining strength behind another shove. Flesh sank deep into the mesh as I tried to drive through to the other side, pain gripping my hands as the thin wires cut into the skin. The screen remained rigid. I fell to the floor, defeated. My drugged brain continued its questioning: Where was I? Why had I been put there? When would I get out? Sleep was the only answer.

When I next awoke, I was still disoriented and weak. Sunlight filtered through the milky pane and the wire screen onto my prone body. Sounds were coming from the hallway. The tile floor had left me stiff. I rolled over and stretched to work out the kinks. In an attempt to stand upright, I crawled to the cot for support, carefully rose onto one knee, then the other. Numbed feet pushed at the floor. The room began to spin around, and around, and around. Strength and balance failed. I crashed back onto the cot.

The door opened. A man carrying a tray tiptoed in, peered at me, swiftly placed the tray on the nightstand, then headed for the door. The door thudded and clicked behind him.

Voices caught my attention. They came from the other side of the door where two faces took turns staring through the small wire window. I strained to get every word of their conversation. They were talking about me.

"He looks quiet enough now."

"Yes, he appears calm."

"He had to be sedated yesterday. There's no family history of insanity, but he can be very aggressive."

"What about his medical history?"

"Anemia. Rheumatic fever. Measles. Minor birth complications. He was a forceps delivery. The forceps severed a nerve in one eye. Some scar tissue. Continued enuretic until age nine. A mild concussion sustained in a car accident at age eleven. Presently undergoing treatment for acute acne vulgaris. A long history of adjustment problems. He's had his share of psychological intervention. Currently a juvenile probationer."

"Anything else?"

"His mother reports that she had him admitted because he displayed signs of deep depression and lethargy. He threatened suicide. Tried it once before, with sleeping pills. What do you think, doctor?"

"I'm not sure. Certainly is a complicated case. Let me review his complete file. We'll have to keep him here until we know more."

"I've been thinking that a series of . . ."

The voices trailed off down the hallway. Had I heard right? Were they going to keep me there? How long? Then what? Would they put me in an institution, like I had been told could happen if I got into more trouble? What was happening to me?

I could no longer hold my anxiety in check. I pressed my face to the small wire window and screamed down the hallway, "Let me outta here! Ya hear me! Let me the hell outta here!"

The sounds of raised voices and hasty footsteps drew toward me.

Again I cried out, "Let me the hell outta here! Bastards! Sons-a-bitches! Let me outta here!"

The hallway was alive with white uniforms. A man moved toward the door, needle in hand.

"Get the hell away from me with that!" I screamed.

The door clicked open. Its movement signaled attack. I grabbed the tray off the nightstand and flung it at the door. The uneaten meal splattered the door, wall, and floor.

The door banged shut. A voice boomed down the hallway, calling for help.

Again the door moved. I grabbed the nightstand and sent it winging. It crashed against the wall next to the door. The door fell back to the security of its lock. I ripped the mattress from the cot and heaved it toward the door, then whirled around to grab something—anything—else to throw. Only the frame of the metal cot remained. In an attempt to break it apart for a weapon, I banged it against the wall, stomped, kicked, and smashed it, yet it held together.

Eyes stared through the small wire window. In a frenzy, I rushed them. The eyes retreated. "Get away from me! I'll kill ya if you come in here!" I raved, throwing my body repeatedly against the door.

I turned to the large screened window and lunged at it. It spit me sprawling to the floor. I charged it again. Fingers ripped and tore at the wire mesh that blocked escape. It would not yield.

I fell to my knees, bawling. Fingernails raked my shoulders and face as I rolled out of control, bleeding. The sound of my screams filled the room.

What happened the next thirty-six hours is not included in the hospital records, nor is it part of my conscious memory. Perhaps, in defense, my brain has forced that information into a corner of my mind where it will remain forever guarded.

When I came back to life, mother was there again, whispering my name. My head was on her soft lap. She rocked and coddled me the way she used to do when I was a baby. I did not have the strength to respond. Heavy eyelids would not stay open. In and out of reality I faded. Deep within me, a frightened child begged, "Hold me, mommy. Don't leave me again. I'm so scared."

Something warm was on my lips. "Drink some of this soup, my baby. You haven't eaten for days. The doctors said you fought everybody who tried to come in here. There, now, I'll take care of you."

As mother continued to soothe me with her voice, faint images toyed with my memory: the endless attacks from the other side of the door; the weakening attempts to stop them. Still, it all seemed unreal—like something from a horror movie where there was terror and pain, but not my own. The tenderness of mother's touch, the warm soup rushing to a hungry stomach and tired body was the only reality. The things of which she spoke seemed foreign, as though they had happened in the distant past or to somebody else.

Soup-fed strength and the passage of time gradually revealed the truth: the condition of the white room, my torn skin, dried blood and burning cuts confirming what I wanted to deny.

Instinctively I clung to mother and sobbed into her breast, "Please, mommy. Please take me home. I don't like this place. I won't cause any more trouble. I'll go to school every day. I won't upset everybody anymore. See, I'm okay now. Please! Please! I'll even go to church if you want. Don't make me stay here. Don't send me away again. I'll be good. You'll see."

Mother listened attentively while I ran endless promises past her, never interrupting or pointing to errors in reasoning. Yet I already knew what I was wishing and what would actually happen were not the same. I could sense it in mother's body, see it in her eyes, feel it in her touch. Even before she spoke, the answer was clear. It would turn out as it always had—worse.

Mother looked down at me. Her eyes were moist, her face pale. She looked, somehow, older. There was sorrow in her voice as she spoke of a place the doctors had recommended, a place where I was to be sent so that I would "get better." I was to be sent to the Harrisburg State Hospital.

Again I pleaded. All my promises and apologies made no difference. Mother would not be swayed. She kept repeating that the state hospital was the best place for me, that she wished it could be otherwise, that she was sorry.

The cell door opened, interrupting mother's regrets. An official-looking man wearing a stiff white coat entered. He introduced himself as my doctor, then asked mother to leave so that he could inform me concerning what to expect at the state hospital.

Mother embraced and kissed me, thanked the doctor, then headed for the door, crying. She turned as she reached the door. "I do love you, my son," she whimpered.

I turned away from her gaze. Her footsteps raced down the hall and away.

2

A House is Not a Home

The memories I retain of family life before the county hospital are distant and confused by emotion. Most of all I remember the heated arguments between father and mother, and father's growing absence. The quarrels became most apparent around the time my brother, Lee, was born, when I was four-and-a-half. Father left us for good near my eleventh birthday, when my sister, Carolyn, entered the world. During those years the quarrels and absences grew increasingly difficult to bear. It was at that time that I began to see the psychologists and psychiatrists. Yet it was not until father formally left us, and my involvement with him became less frequent and more tenuous, that my life finally fell apart.

I don't believe that father ever truly loved me, not in the way a father is supposed to love his son. In fairness to him, however, I cannot remember his being cruel or totally indifferent to me. But neither do I remember his having a meaningful involvement in my life.

While this absence of involvement indicated a lack of emotional commitment to me, there were other events that symbolized the insecurity of our relationship. Like the time he forced me to fight three of the neighborhood boys, one after the other, when he found them pushing me. I had refused to fight back. They beat me rather badly before he stopped it. When I stood before him, shaken, bruised, crying, he offered no comfort. His only response was that he was tired of my being a "momma's boy." There was also the time he drove me to the front of the city orphanage and offered to sign me in when, after one of the many arguments between him and mother, I had voiced my desire to live elsewhere. I was less than nine when both of those events took place. It was then that I began to think I was not the son he wanted.

After father left, I was permitted to see him on Sunday afternoons. I looked forward to those visits; a part-time father was better than no father. But the visits were never quite right. During the two years of strained Sunday afternoons we spent together, father would say bad things about mother. Before and after, mother would say bad things about father. I was caught somewhere in the middle of that war of words, torn apart by the blame they cast at each other through me. One Sunday father had another boy with him. He introduced the boy as a "friend's son," then added that he hoped to marry his "friend" and "adopt" the boy. That is when I decided to stop the Sunday visits. I could see that I had been replaced.

I will always wonder what it was that caused mother and father to fight. Throughout childhood I thought I was in some way responsible since I was the subject of so many of their battles. That guilt worked away inside me for years, twisting my thoughts, feeding my anxiety and surfacing in my behavior.

Now that I have resolved my feelings of guilt, the question that puzzles me most concerns my mother and the origin of what a psychiatrist labeled her "obsessive compulsive neurosis." Did her relationship with father cause it? Or was it her sickness that laid waste to their love? I will never know. All I know is that the neuroses that plagued mother created even more confusion within me and affected my development long after father had gone.

Mother was a pleasure to look at: tall, hourglass figure, oval face, light brown hair, gray eyes. Heads turned when she passed.

She was gentle, too, and kind. To her, faith, hope and charity were rules to live by; God was her strength.

Mother and I were constant companions during childhood. She was very protective of me—too protective some said, especially father. I was always at her side, seldom out of her view. That was her way of shielding me from a recurrence of the rheumatic fever and anemia she believed made me "different" from other children. If it had not been for school, I might never have been allowed to leave the backyard and mother's sight. Even then, for years, I had to come home directly after school so that I would not "get hurt." She even took me to bed with her, on those increasingly frequent nights when father slept elsewhere, so that I would be "safe" with her. And, when father finally left us, mother said that I was the "man of the house." I never questioned her love during that first dozen years; rather, I felt smothered by it.

There was something else about mother's behavior, though, that was even more confusing. She had an overwhelming fear of germs. The problem seemed mild at first, a quirk that could be tolerated, but as the rift between her and father became more extreme so, too, did her war against germs. We had indoor and outdoor clothing. The floor was off limits for play and if our bodies made contact with anything she deemed dirty, we had to be scrubbed clean. Mother believed that rats and insects lived in our house. If a single bug was spied, it was cause for alarm and a thorough cleaning.

After father left and we went to live with mother's parents, her fear of germs became all-consuming. Lysol and ammonia were the weapons she used to ward them off. We had to clean our hands in the disinfectants whenever entering the house. The smell soon covered everything, for she was continually warring against the invasion of germs. Whenever I came home from a Sunday visit with father, a bath in the solution was necessary in order to clean away the filth that he represented.

As much as mother's habit of "crazy cleaning," as she called it, worried and confused me, I still did not question her love—only her odd behavior. But even that remaining thread of stability was soon frayed by doubt. I was twelve and had narrowly managed to pass the seventh grade when a new dilemma arose. Mother decided to place me in a Lutheran Home for orphaned, neglected, and dependent children.

I cried the whole way to the Lutheran Home. It didn't change things, though. Mother kept saying that she was doing what was best for me, that I would like my "new home," and that she would visit "regularly." But her words were no consolation. I clung to her hand during the interview, hoping that my grip would withstand separation. It did not. When mother pulled her hand from mine and headed out the door without me, I felt totally abandoned. First father, then mother, had left me. I had been orphaned.

I was put in a huge old cottage filled with boys. Everybody tried to be friendly, but I only wanted to be left alone to try and understand what had happened. Two of my roommates interrupted my self-imposed solitude, forcing me to wrestle them to see who was "king of the room." I won. They didn't bother me after that. The other boys also eventually left me alone. I ate alone, or didn't eat at all. Whenever possible, I hid: under sheets, in closets, behind bushes, beneath porches, in empty rooms—anywhere and everywhere.

There was an outdoor chapel high on a hill overlooking the Lutheran Home. The altar was made of wood and stone. A double row of wooden benches faced the altar. From the chapel it was possible to see for miles. Few people visited that spot. Those who did could be seen well before they arrived. That was my place. It offered sanctuary. I would pray to God to let me go home and make mother and father love each other again. Then I would cry, knowing that it would never happen.

At the end of the first week, I was given a downtown pass. It seemed the perfect time to run away. I walked down the road thinking about where to go. I had the idea it would be nice to live out on the "lone prairie" with my horse where nobody could hurt me anymore. The plan seemed so good that I called mother and told her. She made me promise not to leave before she said good-bye in person, adding that she would come "directly." I agreed. She never showed. Instead, someone from the Lutheran Home came.

Near the end of my second week, the director of the Lutheran Home called me from crafts class. Mother was waiting in his office. He had phoned and told her that I was not taking advantage of the program, that I was "antisocial" and that there was nothing they could do for me. Mother took me home that day, though I don't think she wanted to. Things were never the same between us after that. I had lost my trust in her and was left to wonder when I would be sent away again.

When father abandoned us, we went to live with mother's parents. Nanan and grandad lived in a semidetached house located only three homes away from where we lived with father. It was a small house: living room, dining room and kitchen on the first floor; three bedrooms and a bath on the second floor. Nanan and grandad each had their own bedrooms. Mother, Lee, Carolyn and I slept in a 10′ × 12′ bedroom where all of our belongings were kept. Lee and I shared a single bed that pressed tightly in a corner of the room. Mother and Carolyn slept in another single bed that was separated from ours by the width of a nightstand. Two dressers and a portable television rounded out the entirety of our furniture. That cramped room was where we were expected to spend the bulk of our time in the house.

At first our living arrangement was bearable. Mother was there to fill our immediate needs, to supervise our activities, to mediate between our desires for play and our grandparents' requests for quiet. When our limited finances became tighter, the atmosphere in the house became increasingly strained. Mother was always fussing about not being able to "make ends meet." According to her, father was constantly behind in his support payments. She was soon forced to find a job. That in itself was a problem. Mother had never worked before. She had barely graduated high school before she was married and I was born. Her only work experience had been that of a housewife and mother. It took her several anxious months before she finally found a position as assistant athletic director at the Y.W.C.A.

The job at the Y did not pay very well, but it provided enough money to meet our limited needs. It also offered an added benefit. Lee, Carolyn, and I were able to spend much of our time with mother at work. Since Carolyn was an infant she almost always accompanied mother to the Y where the women who worked there or used the facilities were pleased to tend or fuss over the "cute baby girl." Lee and I would take a bus to town after school almost every evening that mother worked. On Saturdays we all traveled together to the swimming classes for which mother was responsible. It was a hectic schedule, but well worth it. We were able to be with mother, to remain a family.

After a little more than a year at the Y, mother left to take a better-paying job as a dental assistant. She worked long, erratic hours and we were seldom allowed to visit her. Sometimes we would go to the dentist's office and sit in the waiting room, but that soon came to an end when we were made to realize that the dentist's office was a "place of business," not a "play room." Our involvement with mother outside work was also lessening. She was often tired, sick, upset. I began to miss her very much, as did Lee and Carolyn.

The duty of caring for us fell more and more on the shoulders of our grandparents. They were good people who tried very hard to offer their full support to mother and we three children. Without their meager financial aid we would have been doomed from the very beginning. In the area of emotional aid, however, they were less capable of meeting our needs. The responsibility for overseeing and controlling the daily activities of three children was a tremendous burden for so elderly a couple.

Nanan was nearly seventy years old when we moved under her roof. She was a small woman, barely taller than five feet and weighing no more than one-hundred pounds. Her thinning gray-black hair and deeply wrinkled skin showed the strain of the years of hardship she had endured. Yet there was something in her eyes— an inner strength that even the thick horn-rimmed glasses she wore could not hide. She was a devout Christian and read the Bible daily. Her bedroom was filled with pictures, artifacts, and publications that symbolized her deep commitment to religious ideals. It was through the "grace of God," she believed, that she had managed to overcome life's many obstacles. Indeed, she had done just that. Her life had never been easy. Orphaned at an early age, she had lived in a number of foster homes until adopted. She was trained as a nurse and had worked at a hospital in Fredrick, Maryland, until grandad married her. She had two children: Lee, her first-born, who died at age thirty-six of a rare glandular disease, and mother, who was ten years her brother's junior. Nanan was unquestionably the head of the household. She was the glue that had held her family together during the Great Depression and beyond. Then, in the waning years of her life, when she should have been able to enjoy the peace and contentment of a hard-earned retirement, she was once again called upon to minister to the demands of her daughter and three children. With what remained of her inner strength, she tried to ease our burdens. But the load eventually proved too great.

Grandad was in his mid-sixties, and had just retired from forty years of service on the railroad when we moved in. He was a big man, with wispy black hair that was giving way to baldness. There was a gentleness in his voice and though he was a man of few words, when he chose to speak, people listened. Everybody liked him. There was something in his manner that commanded respect.

Grandad never finished high school. At an early age he went to work to help support his family. The Great Depression almost destroyed him. He refused to take welfare—"hand-outs" as he called it. But when his meager savings were used up, and no other way remained to feed his hungry offspring, he stood in line with the many others. Mother said that he cried on those days because he was ashamed that he was not a better provider.

I loved and admired grandad more than any man I have ever known. He loved me, too, and tried to fill the gap that father had left. When I was very young, grandad would sometimes take me to the railroad yard to ride the trains. The engineers sat me in front with them and gave me special rides. He introduced me to everybody as his "little buddy."

What I remember most about him—the part of his personality that captured my childish imagination—was his love of motorcycles and fishing. Grandad never owned a car. He was a confirmed believer that Harley-Davidson offered the most dependable, economical, and enjoyable form of transportation. Nearly fifty years of motorcycle travel testified to his belief in that philosophy.

Throughout early childhood grandad took me fishing. Those were my happiest days. The night before, we made dough balls for the fish, sandwiches for us. Then we took out grandad's homemade electric worm-digger and vibrated nightcrawlers to the surface, in case the fish were not hungry for dough balls. The next morning we got up before the sun and gathered our fishing gear together. Nanan always made a hearty breakfast for us, to "warm our inners" as grandad said. Then grandad stuffed newspapers inside my coat to "cut the wind," sat me in front of him on the "buddy seat" of "Old Blue," kick-started the big Harley-Davidson, and off we went. The best part of the day was always the ride. Being on that motorcycle, tight against grandad, gave me a special feeling. I was forever waving to people, making them part of my happiness. Sometimes grandad even allowed me to move the pearl-handled gear shift or help him steer. Then, when we got to one of grandad's favorite fishing holes, we unpacked the rods and bait and began to fish. Grandad knew all about fish, especially bass, carp and catfish. He taught me how to trick them onto a hook. We did not talk much on those early morning fishing trips. It was necessary to keep quiet so that we did not scare the fish. But neither fish nor words really mattered to me. Being with grandad, feeling his love, learning the ways of men, were the real importance. On those days I felt whole.

Not long after mother began her job as a dental assistant Nanan's and grandad's positive attitude changed, especially toward me. My behavior grew more disruptive with each incident that represented rejection, separation, or a lack of control over destiny: father's departure, the Lutheran Home, mother's new job. To make matters worse, mother was riddled with ailments: hypoglycemia, panhypopituitaryism, a precancerous lesion, heart problems. There were many times when she lost consciousness, missed work, or had to be hospitalized due to her ailments, and it was not uncommon for her to be so tired, drugged or ill that even though she was in the house, it was as if she was not there at all. But she was not the only one who suffered from sickness. Leukemia was slowly eating away at grandad. Nanan had heart problems. I could not fully understand what was occurring, except to feel I was somehow losing them and to fear what might happen. Fear further aggravated my negative behavior while guilt over not being able to help them deepened my confusion.

As time went on, mother became less accessible, grandad began to spend more time in his garage workshop or sitting silently by the front window staring through cigarette smoke, and Nanan was left with the burden of controlling three children as well as worrying over and ministering to the needs of her sick husband and daughter. Swamped by the responsibility for holding everything together, her nerves shot, her patience gone, she turned to me with her awesome load believing that, as the eldest child, I would be able to provide some support. I could not deliver. Instead, my

behavioral problems grew in direct response to the increased difficulties, further inflaming the situation. It was not long before Nanan
took her anguish out on me. She began to scold or blame me for
everything. She told me I was "in league with the devil," responsible
for "worrying everybody sick," always "causing too much commotion," and she claimed my acne was "the evil trying to get out" of me.
More and more I began to believe all the problems plaguing that
house were my fault. I began to run away and stay out until late at
night rather than be the cause of further problems or watch the pain
that was tearing us apart.

3

School Days

In many ways school reflected the ebb and flow of my problems at home. As early as the first grade, a teacher considered my conduct sufficiently "moody" to advise that I be taken to a child guidance counselor. The remainder of the primary grades brought no other extraordinary difficulties. I got along well with classmates, created no disciplinary problems, and managed average grades. It was not until the seventh grade that my school performance showed the full effect of what had been happening to me.

The summer before entering junior high school I was consumed by the thought that I would die before school began. The sense of forboding I felt resulted not only from family problems but from a dwindling self-confidence in all areas of my life that made me dread the prospect of meeting new students who might criticize my appearance and exceed my academic performance. My fears proved prophetic. Though I did not die in the literal sense, my school involvement was lifeless. I could not keep my mind on the subjects. I was too involved with the home predicament. The new students tolerated my presence, but I made no new friends. Although the year ended with a report card filled with F's, I was passed, nonetheless.

The next year I was placed in a special education class. Several of my new classmates were old enough to drive. A few were unable to spell their names. The rest performed little better. Students in other classes called us names like "hoods" or the "dummy section." We had cleats on our shoes, wore our collars up, and combed our greasy hair into "ducktails." Between classes we stood in the hallway where we called people names, made obscene gestures, tried to start fights. We were not allowed to move from classroom to classroom like the other students. The principal visited us often. I managed a B average.

When I was halfway through the eighth grade, the administration decided to place me in a more advanced class. Though the level of work was not that much greater, my grades dropped like a stone. I felt like a ping-pong ball being bounced from one learning environment to another. I was absent from school thirty-seven days. What had formerly been a solid B average fell to slightly above a C. I passed the grade.

Freshman year proved to be my ultimate academic downfall. For some reason that to this day still puzzles me, I was put in an accelerated college preparatory grouping. Classes like Latin and algebra totally eluded me. I flunked them both and received a C in English, a C in science, a D in history, and an "unsatisfactory" in art. I was absent thirteen days, tardy three times, and piled up an incredible amount of detention time for disciplinary reasons. Socially I fared no better. My face and neck were plagued by giant pus-producing sores that often burst in class and left bloody scabs. Nervous tics displayed further inner turmoil. The hand-me-down and bargain-basement clothes I wore were a stark contrast to the tailored, brand-name outfits worn by my well-kempt fellow students. Classmates barely acknowledged my existence. At this point I had begun to expect failure and rejection. The year had to be repeated.

The second year in ninth grade I was assigned to an academic level more consistent with my abilities. The course work was less demanding, the other students less achievement-oriented. It should have been an appropriate educational experience. Unfortunately,

however, it did not turn out that way. The shame of repeated scholastic and social failure spurred me to seek recognition in any form
possible. Rebellion became the focus of my new identity.

The year began on a symbolic note. The first day of school a
student who was a tackle on the junior high varsity football team
and considered to be the toughest kid in our homeroom tried to
provoke me into a fight. He shoved and called me names. At first I
tried to ignore him, but when he kept it up, I pushed him over a
desk and jumped on top of him. He quickly apologized. The other
students congratulated me for beating the class bully. The teacher
gave me two hours of detention. Respect from the other students
outweighed the punishment.

A few months later, I got into trouble with the art teacher. I
was sitting at the same table with Rusty, one of the boys in the gang
I had begun to loaf with after school, and we were screwing around
instead of doing our assigned projects. The teacher told us to
"knock it off." We quieted down for a while, then got to clowning
again. The teacher yelled at us a second time and when Rusty ut-
tered a four-letter word, the teacher threatened to smack him. I
could not allow something like that to happen to a pal. Everybody
in our gang had sworn an oath to stick together. I reached for the
knife that I had begun to carry, flicked it open under the table, and
handed it to Rusty. I doubt that the teacher saw the knife but some
of the students did. The teacher sent Rusty to the office. Before he
left, Rusty handed back the knife under the table and I pocketed it,
assuming a pose of innocence.

By then the whole class was buffaloed. They began to take
orders from me. I liked to have them stand by their seats at attention; then, upon my command, they would sit in unison. When the
civics teacher saw this routine he screamed that we were behaving
"like a bunch of ants." Everybody turned to me. I was on the spot.
"Ants are smart," I countered. That really upset him. He started
down the aisle, hands clenched, a nasty look in his eyes. I thought

he was going to hit me and I jumped up to face him. He stopped and back-tracked to the front of the room, pointing toward the principal's office. The principal gave me more detention and said that if there was any more trouble I would be expelled.

The one teacher who would not allow any disruption in his class was Mr. Peters, my math and homeroom teacher and the football coach. I always laid low around him, aware that he was nobody to tangle with. But one day I made a mistake. Mike Gallagher and I were seated near the rear of the room. We were playing "flinch" while Mr. Peters chalked math problems on the blackboard. I had just caused Mike to flinch by faking a punch at his face. Since he had blinked and moved his head, I had earned the right to punch his arm. I hit him squarely on the meaty part. The sound echoed throughout the room. Everybody heard it, including Mr. Peters. He turned to see the entire class staring at me, dropped the chalk in the tray and motioned me outside the room. The class watched silently as I slunk down the aisle, out the door. Mr. Peters grabbed me by the shirt, slammed me against the wall, and slapped my face. His only words were, "Get back to your seat and straighten up."

My first impulse was to knee him in the groin. The incident was bound to harm my reputation since the class had to know what had happened. I did not want them to lose their respect for me. The more I thought about it, though, the smarter it seemed to do precisely as he said. If I did not drop him with the first shot, he would wipe the floor with me, and if he did fall, I would still be in trouble. There was no winning. Besides, I respected the way he handled the situation. He had not slapped me in front of the class, which would have really put me on the spot. I did as he said and never again caused trouble in his presence.

Even though I had "learned a lesson" from Mr. Peters, I continued my disruptive behavior in other classes, soon piling up so many infractions that I became a regular member of the after-school detention hall. My reputation spread throughout the school until not only the students but the staff and administration came to regard me as a troublemaker.

Within two weeks of the hassle with Mr. Peters, I was once again involved in a physical confrontation. It happened during lunch period. I was seated in the lobby, watching some of the other students dance, when Jerry Klein came over to me and said, "I hear you think you're tough!" I did not reply. Jerry was one of the roughest kids in ninth grade. "Hey, punk! Didn't you hear me?" he shouted. When I looked away, hoping to avoid the fight, he pulled me off the chair and punched me square on the face, hitting a sore pimple. Pain shot through my body. Everything turned red. I grabbed his neck and beat his head against a door. I kept bouncing him off the door until several students pulled us apart. Jerry was carried to the nurses' room. I was escorted to the principal's office. The principal did not listen to my side of the story. He just shook his head and kept repeating: "You really did it this time." Then he suspended me and called the Juvenile Probation Office. Jerry got off with a warning.

Suspension meant I was not allowed to attend public school, but the law dictated that participation in an eduational program was mandatory for minors. Since the juvenile court had become involved in the matter, and since there was no alternative educational experience available, I was placed in the county detention center, where classes were held, until I could be reinstated in the home school district. Confinement in the detention center served to confirm my growing negative self-image. I was not even wanted at school.

It was a gloomy day, indeed, when mother took me to the county court house to meet Mr. Lantz, the chief probation officer. He talked with mother, then me, explaining why I must be put in the detention center until a juvenile court hearing was convened and a judge could determine my disposition. Mr. Lantz then escorted me to the detention center and left me there. Once again I felt as though the whole world was rejecting me, confirming my belief that I was "no good."

The detention center was an old, four-story brick building that had seen better days and occupants other than delinquent children. In the rear was a small play area, bordered by a high, wire fence. A kitchen, dining room, waiting room, office, and recreational area filled the long, narrow first floor. The second floor had an apartment for the houseparents who supervised our daily activities. The third floor was comprised of two large rooms filled with chicken-wire cages containing a single cot and locker. It was in these cages that we slept. We were also put in them when there was nothing to do or as punishment. The cages were always locked when we were put inside. Above us on the fourth floor were the two small rooms used for the school.

I spent the first day padlocked inside one of the chicken-wire cages. The only time I was allowed to leave was when one of the houseparents came to take me to the toilet. Meals were brought by tray and slid under the door. Since there were no books, magazines, or toys for diversion, I could only walk the short length of the cage or lie on the cot and question my predicament. Was I really such a "bad" child? What would happen in juvenile court? Was I to be sent to prison as Nanan had suggested might occur if my behavior did not improve? Did the whole world hate me? A steady stream of questions buffeted me. I could find no meaningful answers.

After the first day of isolation I was allowed to mingle with the other kids. Less than a dozen of us made up the entire population. We all looked the same: sad, lost, confused, worried about what disaster tomorrow might bring. Family problems were often at the core of each life story we exchanged. Some stayed to themselves. Others constantly pushed, shoved, taunted, or fought whoever was available, transferring their pain to someone else. A few left for court, never to be seen by us again. New faces replaced them.

On weekdays we attended school. There was only one teacher

to oversee our activities and assign lessons. But it was all just a joke. Magazines, comic books, and old torn texts that had been abandoned by public schools were used as the means of instruction. Using the *Adventures of Superman* seemed a strange way to teach English. Mostly, the teacher tried to keep us from tearing the place, and each other, apart. The moment his attention turned to the questions of one student, several others would get into a ruckus. Nobody could or would study under such conditions.

After school and on the weekend those of us who were not being punished for some indiscretion, and thus stuck in a cage, were sent to the recreation room, where there was little to do. Only a television and some reading materials were available in the sparsely furnished room and we were soon at each other's throats, acting out our discontent. Sometimes we were allowed to play in the fenced rear yard. But the games often turned into free-for-alls or arguments. The cages were where we spent most of the time, locked away like wild animals. We acted as we felt.

There were few interruptions from the boredom of the daily schedule of school, recreation, cage. Mother came to visit several times. She always left crying. Grandad came once but did not know what to say. The look in his eyes said enough. I could see his sorrow and the helplessness he felt in not being able to change the situation. Mr. Lantz came twice. Each visit was a question-and-answer session with him hunched over the table writing volumes of notes as we talked. Our eyes seldom met.

The monotonous uncertainty continued ten days. Then, on the morning of the eleventh day, the waiting ended. Mr. Lantz came and escorted me to the York County Court House, where I was to meet a judge who would determine my fate. I was sure that I would be sent to the prison at White Hill.

4

A Day in Court

There was silence in the room as mother, Mr. Lantz, Mr. Detweiler, and I sat awaiting the judge's arrival. Mother looked at the floor and wound and rewound a Kleenex. Mr. Detweiler stared silently ahead, hands folded, his thumbs drawing invisible circles around one another. Mr. Lantz continually scanned a pile of papers. I searched each of their faces for a clue. They avoided my gaze.

The door opened. A man and a woman entered. Everybody stood. The man sat behind a desk and the woman took her place behind a dictating machine. My throat went dry as I stared at the neatly dressed old man who would judge me.

"Please be seated," the judge began.

We obeyed.

The following is a transcription of the proceedings.

Henry Lantz, called as a witness and duly sworn, testified as follows:

"Judge Arkins, we are asking you to interest yourself in Waln Karl Brown who is coming to court this afternoon on our petition, the substance of which is that Dr. David Yale, Mr. C. S. Detweiler and his mother have informed us that this boy is incorrigible. For several weeks prior to April 4, 1960, he refused to obey the reasonable and lawful com-

mands of his family. Recently he engaged in a fight at
school and was suspended. Mr. Detweiler very kindly con-
sented to come to court this afternoon and to personally
advise the court as to the school's experience with Waln."

Mr. Detweiler, called as a witness and duly sworn, testified as follows:

By the Court:

Q. "All right, I will hear from you first, Mr. Detweiler."

A. "In the beginning of the year Waln started with average
attendance, I would say, and did fair work. He was repeating the grade. As the time went on a bit, we had a problem
with attendance and from the opening of school, which was
September 9, to January 18, we have an absenteeism of
nineteen and one-half days. It is our practice at school to
contact the home every time someone is absent, and I had
a report from the home that Waln was probably well
enough to come to school but simply refused to come to
school. That was from his grandparents. At the same time I
contacted Mrs. Brown and she said, 'I can't make the boy
go to school, he just refuses to go to school.' I contacted
Mr. Lantz at the same time and he said, 'Well, it's either one
of two things, either he attends school or he will have to
be under my jurisdiction.' At that time I got in touch with
Waln personally, myself, and I told him it's either come to
school or he will be turned over to the detention authorities. Waln responded at that time and came to school. It
was with the understanding, he would either be at school
at 11:00 or he would be taken to the Detention Home, but
Waln came. Soon after that Waln's grades commenced to
drop off considerably, very noticeably. When he was called

into our Guidance Counselor's office, inquiring about it, to
see what to do about it, his answer constantly would be,
'Well, I don't know how long I'm going to be around, I feel
I won't be in school very long and it's just no use working.'
The report cards were issued on the 23rd of March and
Wednesday Waln did not go home, instead of that he left
and was truant from school, as well as from home, for the
next two days. When he did come back to school the beginning of the following week, on the 29th, somehow or
other he got mixed up with another boy in school for
which I suspended him from school. I told Mr. Lantz that I
feel we can't do very much for him because he expressed
to our Guidance Counselor and to myself that he was unhappy with his home. In fact, he told us on many occasions
he did not go home from school but he would go some
other place and loafed around and maybe around 9:00 or
9:30 he would come home and go immediately to his
room. When we asked him what he did for meals, well, if he
had money he would buy something at the store or go
without. I can only say that I believe if he were somewhere
where there would be continual guidance and supervision
he probably would have a chance to become a good citizen. But he has not demonstrated that for us."

Q. "When were the last grades issued at school?"

A. "The last grades for him were issued March 23rd."

Q. "Do you know what those grades were?"

A. "We have a marking, I don't know exactly, we have a
marking of 5, 4, 3, 2, 1, and 2 is passing and 1 is failing, and
I believe he had three 1's in a major subject. The last report
card was the very worst one, he simply gave up. We carry
four majors and I think he was passing one, as I recall."

Mrs. Brown, called as a witness and duly sworn, testified as follows:

Q. "Mrs. Brown, I would like to hear your analysis of this
problem."

A. "He is from a broken home and he suffers a lot because
of it. We live with my parents who are well up in years. My
mother will be 73 in December and I am afraid they are
not well equipped to cope with three young children, because of our finances—I have to work to help support the
home and it doesn't leave me very much time to be all the
things I would like to be with the children. I have had Dr.
Yale involved on a number of occasions, I have consulted
him, and I had Waln see him. Waln lived through a pretty
unbearable period for the last four or five years. He has a
great deal of ability. I do feel he is emotionally disturbed as
the result of all that he's been put through."

Waln Karl Brown, called as a witness and duly sworn,
testified as follows:

By the Court:

Q. "Waln, I would like to hear your analysis of this matter."

A. "Well, the reason I didn't do my school work, I thought
I was going to be sent to White Hill."

Q. "Who gave you that impression?"

A. "My grandparents."

Q. "How long have you thought that?"

A. "About a month and a half, something like that, maybe it
wasn't that long, I'm not sure."

Q. "Well, unless you stopped working completely, I don't see how your grades could have fallen to the point they now are in that short a time."

A. "I didn't stop working completely. The last marking period I got 4, 3, 2, and two 1's."

Q. "In what did you have the 4?"

A. "Math."

Q. "What math?"

A. "General business."

Q. "And the 3?"

A. "In English."

Q. "In what did you have the 2?"

A. "Typing."

Q. "What do you do after school?"

A. "I come home, then I usually might change pants or something like that, then I go up—we have this garage where we fix motorcycles and stuff."

Q. "Who has that?"

A. "It's a group of us boys around there."

Q. "Where is it?"

A. "You know where the Pensupreme Store is? You know where the Lincoln Highway Garage is?"

Q. "Yes."

A. "Right around that, catercorner to that."

Q. "How many fellows are in that group?"

A. "I don't know, it's about eight of us, something like that."

Q. "Do most of them have motorcycles, things of that nature?"

A. "There's only about two, the rest we're just fixing them up, almost all are sixteen or just about close to it."

Q. "If there are only two motorcycles, they would not require a great deal of work."

A. "No, there's four motorcycles and a motorbike."

Q. "Even so, if you have to work on them everyday, they must require a lot of work."

A. "Well, sometimes we work, you know, a generator is gone sometimes, something like that and we build it from scratch. We buy a piece of junk that's all rusted and stuff and we fix it up."

Q. "What seems to be the situation at home?"

A. "Well, we stay with my grandparents."

Q. "You seem to feel you don't like it at home. What happens there that you don't like?"

A. "Well, they yell at me and stuff like that, so I don't stay around."

Q. "What do they yell at you about?"

A. "Anything I do. If I walk in the front door or something like that."

Q. "You mean as soon as you walk in the front door somebody yells at you?"

A. "No, like if I walk in the front door, she says, 'Well, there he goes again,' and then she says she told me a million times not to walk there."

Q. "Where are you supposed to walk?"

A. "I am supposed to go around the back way and take off my shoes."

Q. "You mean you have to walk in the house in your stocking feet?"

A. "Either that or wipe them off, so I just go to my room and watch television, something like that."

Q. "You think that's a big job of cleaning off your shoes before going in the house?"

A. "No."

Q. "What do you think you would like to do when you finish high school?"

A. "I'm not too sure. I would like to work on cars, something like that, or maybe skin dive."

Q. "There doesn't appear to be much connection between skin diving and working on cars."

A. "I like mechanics and stuff like that. Next year if I am around, I'm going to see if I can take the academic course at York High, and I like swimming a lot."

Q. "You don't expect to get much experience working on cars in an academic course?"

A. "Well, industrial—I don't know what it is—they have machines to work on, I'm not sure what it is. Car mechanics, something."

Q. "According to all the tests you have had, your ability is rather high which indicates to me you have been doing very little in school, and the fact that you say you quit working because about a month or six weeks ago you got the idea you might be sent to the prison at White Hill, your school work began to decline in quality, yet you are repeating a grade apparently you did not pass last year."

A. "That's true. I had Algebra and Latin and I didn't understand it."

Q. "Your ability would tend to indicate to me college preparatory should not present any difficulty problems, if you applied yourself to it."

A. "I tried it but I couldn't understand it, I just couldn't get it."

Q. "I would say either you were not working sufficiently or something was wrong with the instruction. I am not in position to say at this point which it is or whether it might be a combination of both, but with the ability you evidently have, even with poor instruction, you shouldn't have trouble passing even a college preparatory course if you work. Do you think you really would work?"

A. "Yes."

Q. "How much time do you spend studying outside of school hours?"

A. "Do you mean last year or this year?"

Q. "Both."

A. "I didn't do too much this year. Last year I spent about an hour every night."

Q. "Well, that's not enough."

A. "Then sometimes I would stay up until 1:00.

Q. "But what time would you start?"

A. "About 6:00 or 7:00."

Q. "You mean you studied from 6:00 to 1:00?"

A. "I did reports and stuff."

Q. "How frequently did you do that? I mean from 6:00 in the evening to 1:00 in the morning."

A. "Oh, once a week or once every two weeks."

Q. "You studied continuously for several hours?"

A. "Yes. Like if we had to do a chapter on plants, I would look up all the stuff I could find about it and write a report."

Q. "I am satisfied, Waln, the circumstances under which you have been living have not been normal. However, at the same time I am not satisfied that you have done everything within your power to cope with those circumstances. Why did you and James Hartman go to Baltimore?"

A. "I didn't want to be sent to White Hill."

Q. "Don't you think that is a pretty good way of getting sent there?"

A. "I didn't think I was going to come back."

Q. "Where did you think you were going?"

A. "Florida."

Q. "What were you going to do when you got there?"

A. "I don't know. I was told that you can drive when you are fifteen down there."

Q. "Well, I am not going to send you to White Hill, I am not going to send you anywhere right now. If I do send you anywhere, it won't be to White Hill.

A. "That's what my grandparents kept saying, I was going to be sent to White Hill."

Q. "I am telling you now you will not be sent to White Hill and you will not be sent anywhere at the moment, but if in the future I should determine it might be necessary to send you somewhere, it will not be to White Hill, but I am not going to say you will not, perhaps, spend some time in some institution somewhere. Now, whether you do or whether you don't is going to depend almost a hundred per cent on you. If you get any more ideas about taking off, going to Baltimore or anywhere else like that and run away, that is about the best way I know to commit yourself to an institution. Now, if you were not able to do the work at school, I would feel much more sympathetic to your difficulties at school. I am thoroughly convinced if you apply yourself properly you can get not only passing but substantially good grades in your school work. You tell me you spend an hour outside of school hours on your work, I tell you that is not enough even for a boy of your ability, if he wants to do good work. On the other hand, if you do conscientious work in school during hours, there is absolutely no reason for you ever to have to spend seven hours in one night on school work. I have no objection to your going to the garage and working with other boys on motorbikes and motorcycles, if you get pleasure out of that, but I want to see you go back to school and I don't want to see you getting in any further difficulty there. Now, your mother has indicated you are somewhat athletically inclined. Have you ever tried out for any athletic teams?"

A. "Not in school."

Q. "Why not?"

A. "I was on the swim team at the Y."

Q. "Why didn't you go in for some athletics at school?"

A. "I didn't want to stay after school."

Q. "Why not?"

A. "I wanted to go home."

Q. "Now, you tell me in one breath you want to get home and a few breaths before that you tell me you didn't like to go home."

A. "No, I mean I wanted to get out and play and stuff, I didn't want to stay at school."

Q. "How do you know you are good at athletics if you didn't participate in them?"

A. "I used to."

Q. "When?"

A. "When I was in the sixth grade."

Q. "What kind of athletics?"

A. "Well, if they had a track team, I would be on that; I would swim."

Q. "What did you do on the track team?"

A. "I was in everything for our school."

Q. "Well, what events did you participate in?"

A. "Softball throw."

Q. "I am talking about track."

A. "Yes, softball throw, high jump, broad jump, and running."

Q. "What did you run?"

A. "The 50-yard dash."

Q. "What was your best time?"

A. "I don't remember—seven or eight seconds or so."

Q. "How high did you go on the high jump?"

A. "I don't remember that. That was in the sixth grade."

Q. "Well, I understand that."

A. "Around five feet, I guess, four, I don't remember. It was the best one."

Q. "How far was your farthest broad jump?"

A. "I don't remember that either."

Q. "Well, athletics take work, the same as anything else. If you are going to make your living on automobiles, you will have to work, you will work eight hours a day, at least five days a week, and it is not easy work."

The Court: "Is his suspension from school in effect?"

Mr. Detweiler: "No, it was a three-day suspension."

Q. "How long have you been in the Detention Home now?"

A. "Last Monday I was in."

Q. "You mean Monday of this week?"

A. "No, last week."

Q. "You have been there a week and four days?"

A. "Yes."

Q. "Did you have any difficulty getting along with people up there?"

A. "No."

The Court: "In this case we find there have been acts of delinquency, principally truancy from school.

"Accordingly, we enter this order.

"And now, to wit, April 14, 1960, upon consideration of the testimony presented, it is ordered, adjudged and decreed that Waln Karl Brown has committed acts of delinquency, particularly truancy and running away, he is, therefore, adjudged a delinquent youth in need of the care of this court, for the time being he is placed on probation in the custody of his mother, with the understanding that he will regularly attend school, that he will obey the reasonable commands of his mother, that he will make a serious effort to satisfactorily perform the work that is required by his various school assignments; we direct that he be returned to court as soon as practicable after the termination of the current school term at which time we will review his progress."

5

Street Life

Adjudication heightened my image of myself as a "good-for-nothing" child. Having a probation officer made me feel like a criminal. My outsider role grew increasingly more defined. There seemed to be no place where I fit. There were other boys who, like me, did not seem to fit, and it was toward them that I gravitated in order to establish a sense of belonging. We had banded together over the years, one by one, to create a small gang. There were six of us comprising the core of the group, though others came and went or were only part-time participants. We six were constantly together when the school day did not separate us. We drew strength from each other. The street was our home.

James was the leader. A doctor's son, he was the most assertive, best-looking, but not the toughest, member of our gang. His pockets were always filled with money stolen from or given to him by his parents. We often took the Porsche Roadster that was his father's and drove it through the alleys. James was not old enough to have a driver's license, but that did not stop him from showing us how marvelously the car handled. Wherever we went, whatever we did, James always picked up the tab, treating us to horseback rides, movies, bowling, pinball, and food. His basement playroom was filled with every form of toy and game designed to capture the imagination of any teenage boy. His clothes were the newest fashion and best brands. There seemed to be nothing he did not have. He was the envy of us all. Along with me, he had failed the ninth grade. His father was never at home. His mother never left the house.

Greg Keller was the oldest, biggest, and toughest. His broken nose and fireplug build gave him the look of a fighter. He was always dressed poorly, wearing work-boots and hand-me-down clothes passed on by an older brother. His home was no larger than an oversized garage. We seldom saw his mother and were never permitted inside the house. His father was a truck driver, on the road constantly. There were always several scrapped Kaiser automobiles at the rear of the house which his father cannibalized for parts to keep one car running. Greg was a genius at all things mechanical. He could tear down and rebuild any engine, ride a bicycle on its back wheel for a city block, do tricks on a motorcycle—and he had a drivers license. He was our hero. Greg had failed at least two grades.

Jack Smythe was the most intelligent. He did well in school, was in the accelerated academic program, the only one in our gang who never failed a grade. We were best friends since before elementary school and had been in the same classrooms until junior high, when we were separated by placement in different groupings. Jack's family was well-to-do. Somebody was always dying and leaving them more money. T. P., his older brother by five years, terrorized the neighborhood by setting off rockets, firecrackers, and various explosives he concocted in his basement laboratory. Jack's father sold real estate and was on-the-go all day, almost every day of the week. His mother drank martinis from morning to night. Jack was not always with us. He spent many hours studying, experimenting in the basement laboratory, practicing the accordion, attending social functions. His level-headedness was admired. We all turned to him for advice and counsel.

Rusty Reese was the most aggressive, ready to fight at the slightest remark he perceived as threatening. His father was a large man who had gained some recognition as a football player but had had to settle for a job as salesman when he failed to make the pros. His mother was also large and wore long-sleeved dresses and blouses and sat around with a glazed smile on her face. The one time that I saw her arms, there were many small red holes in them. Empty beer cans littered the house. Rusty's older sister was always with a different guy. Her dates gave us coins to leave the room while they kissed and touched her body. His younger brother was a "holy terror." Rusty had flunked school twice and been suspended more than once. His parents sometimes beat him. He was a perpetual companion, spending almost every waking minute away from home.

Theodore Davenport III, called "Dobey" for short, was a late arrival to our gang. A chubby boy who was destined to be fat, he looked out of place no matter what he wore. He was the butt of our jokes. Though I preferred to view myself as better off than him, he and I had many things in common: his parents were divorced, he was on probation, and he had failed a grade. He lived in a small walk-up apartment with his heavyset mother. When he turned sixteen, he quit school and lost job after job. He was always to be found in one of our hangouts. Dobey tried to act tough, though he could not pull it off. At Christmas and on birthdays he gave away tokens of affection.

It was with these five boys that I spent my happiest times, the problems at home, school, and elsewhere magically disappearing in the spontaneity of play, which made life momentarily more like I wished it to be: free, easy, relatively controllable. Friendship allowed me to become a part of something that failed me in all other areas of life. With them I did not feel like an outcast. A sympathetic ear tuned to a common pain or worry made some difficulties more bearable. We were a family unto ourselves and shared many adventures.

Engines were one of our mutual interests. When we tired of

bicycles, we took up motorbikes, designing and constructing them ourselves, though Greg did most of the mechanical work. A three horsepower engine attached to an old bicycle frame made a nifty vehicle. Those belt-driven motorbikes had the barest essentials: small gas tank, hand clutch, front hand brake, throttle. The pedal assembly, chain and rear brake were removed and a piece of metal or wood was wedged in the hole where the pedal assembly had been, producing motorcycle-like footrests. There was no rear brake. A few of us had speedometers mounted on the handlebars. Speeds exceeding forty miles per hour were recorded. They were a source of great fun, but very dangerous. We all took our lumps as a result of spills. Many a pair of shoes were worn through from the do-it-yourself braking. We terrorized the neighborhood on our illegal machines, kicking over garbage cans, tearing up yards, knocking other kids off bicycles, and frightening motorists who came to skidding stops in an attempt to avoid hitting us. The baffleless mufflers made a thunderous roar that irritated adults. Though the police constantly chased us, we always escaped.

Pinball was another group activity. We spent a large amount of time and money trying to beat the machines. A cigar store was our favorite hang-out because it had the best machine and, although it was illegal, paid off for games won. We met there almost every evening after school, put our money into a group kitty, and played until we—or our funds—were exhausted.

There were other boys who also hung out at the cigar store. Some were loners. Many were members of a gang called the Dragon Deuces. When we first began to frequent the cigar store, some of the older boys used to shove us and tilt the machine when we played. We soon grew tired of being pushed around. We bought gravity knives, filed their catches, and put graphite on the blades so that they opened and locked into place with a flick of the wrist. A few threats with the improvised switchblades brought us respect and acceptance. Everybody quit picking on us.

It was not long before we began to loaf with the Dragon Deuces. Some of them had customized cars with high-powered engines and took us along on rides through town where they drag-raced between stoplights. Sometimes they had us start fights with other gangs so that they could jump in. The Dragon Deuces liked to "rumble." It gave us a real sense of power to be associated with them. We were soon copying their every move, hoping to be just like them.

There was a small park adjacent to the cigar store where we spent some of our time. The Dragon Deuces considered the park their "turf." As our gang became more involved with them, we started to defend the park against rival gangs. One day we decided to chase off a group of young blacks who were playing football in the park. That night they returned en masse. About twenty of us stood in the dim moonlight, armed with knives, hammers, chains, metal rods, and other weapons. The police came just as we were about to fight. Everybody went home. The next day a solidly-built black kid found me in the park and asked if I had been involved in the ruckus. I answered "Yes" with pride. He flipped me onto the ground, straddled my chest, and asked if I wanted to continue. I said "No way." We became fast friends.

Not all problems were so easily resolved. As the tensions at home and school grew more difficult to handle, I turned increasingly to the streets in search of relief. Yet even they seemed too confining, too close to the source of the tensions. If I was to survive, I needed a more definite solution, an ultimate escape.

At this point James, too, was upset by home problems. Though I do not remember the exact causes, the effects were clear: he seldom went home for meals, stayed on the streets longer than any of us, and stole more and more money from his parents. It did not take us long to agree on a plan to run away. Florida was our destination. We would leave after school.

The late winter wind was cold on that March evening when we

met by the railroad tracks. Both James and I had stolen money from our families, though his amount far exceeded mine. We headed south along the tracks knowing the police would search the roads for us. We hoped to hop a train and ride the whole way. At first it was a game—balancing on the rails, matching strides with the varied widths of the cross ties. But the fun soon ceased: night closed in, our bellies grumbled, the cold wind cut to the bone, no trains showed. We huddled together by the tracks, exhausted, and waited for sunrise. We could not sleep. At daybreak we set off without enthusiasm. Our steps were less sure, more labored. The miles dragged by. When it seemed impossible to go further, we rented a room in a cheap hotel and went to a diner where we overheard two policemen talking about two runaway boys. Our hamburgers went unfinished. We quickly paid the cashier and headed back in the direction from which we had come. Early the next morning, I staggered through the front door and fell asleep on the sofa.

It was after that failed attempt at escape that life came apart at the seams: school became more difficult to bear, detention time accumulated, absenteeism increased, the fight with Jerry took place; then: suspension, the detention home, the court hearing, adjudication, probation. Everybody was watching and waiting for my next mistake. Mr. Detweiler checked on me at school, the teachers observed every move in class, Nanan preached the Gospel, mother reported countless mistakes, and Mr. Lantz recorded everything.

6

A Probation Officer's
Point of View

The experiences thus far related are taken from memory. In order to add a further dimension regarding my delinquent adaptation and to review the circumstances which led to June 8, 1960, and my subsequent hospitalization, the probation officer's report and probation hearing records are included. Though I do not agree with or remember every entry, and though there is a certain amount of redundancy, I am presenting Mr. Lantz's recorded comments verbatim because they offer the observations of a perceptive professional who proved to be far more attuned to the situation than I realized at the time.

PROBATION OFFICER'S REPORT

Waln Karl Brown   Hon. George W. Arkins
(Juv-Del) Incorrigibility   Probation
April 14, 1960

Jurisdiction

Waln Karl Brown, age 15, was born on October 14, 1944, at the York Hospital, York, Pennsylvania. His birth certificate has been verified through examination of York Hospital certificate #2051A. Currently Waln is residing with his separated mother, Mrs. Louise (Strine) Brown, and her parents, Mr. and Mrs. Elmer Strine, at their home in York, Pennsylvania.

Complaint

The complaints against this boy were made by his mother, Dr. Yale, at the York Mental Health Center, and Mr. C. S. Detweiler, High School Principal, to the effect that Waln was incorrigible, in that he refused to obey the reasonable and lawful commands of his family, that he is emotionally disturbed and that recently he engaged in a fight at school and was suspended.

Placement in Detention

Waln was accompanied to the detention home on Monday morning, April 4, 1960.

Previous Complaints

In January, 1959, Dr. Yale, psychologist at the York Mental Health Center, referred Waln to the probation office, as it was his feeling that something ought to be done with his home situation. He characterized Waln as being very emotionally disturbed. He said some of this was probably due to the mother.

About the same time Mrs. Brown came to the office and complained in a very unusual manner about her son's behavior. The substance of her complaint was that the boy was tormenting the maternal grandparents with whom she lived, carrying on at school so as to worry her, doing things that were going to make him flunk his year at school, that he was headstrong and refused to obey her reasonable and lawful commands. We got the impression that Mrs. Brown was so filled with anxiety over her own separation from the boy's father that she was confusing her own problems with those of her son. At that time we suggested that she confer with a local psychiatrist, as we felt she could use and was badly in need of therapeutic help. We also saw Waln and found him not to be as disturbed as his mother made him out to be. A workable plan was suggested to the boy and he readily agreed to follow through with it. The matter was handled unofficially.

Family Situation

Since our original contact with the Brown family we have heard rumblings of trouble in the household. It seems that Mr. and Mrs. Brown were married when Mrs. Brown was but seventeen years of age and largely at her insistence. Mr. Brown was young and had an orchestra. He lived across the street from the Strines. He became attracted to her and later the marriage was consummated. At the time Mr. Brown worked at a Safe and Lock company and continued his employment during the war. Mrs. Brown continued with her schooling and finally graduated. For about thirteen years they argued and fought. About ten years ago Mrs. Brown wanted a divorce. Mr. Brown demurred, as he wanted to keep the family intact. It seems that in 1956, when Mr. Brown was called to California to drive a sickly uncle back home, he took Waln with him. From then on things became so acute that he finally left the home and moved to his parents' home, which is approximately one block away.

Subsequently Waln's mother claimed that he was running around with other women. Mr. Brown denied this.

After their last child, Carolyn Kathleen, was born on October 15, 1955, Mr. Brown had reached a point in his life where he could not stand Mrs. Brown's interference and he told her he did not love her any more. Nevertheless, he bought a new place and tried to make a fresh start. This proved unsuccessful and later Mrs. Brown consulted an attorney and Mr. Brown did likewise. Subsequently he lost the house, lost the respect and love of his children, and since then he has been contributing various amounts of money to the care and maintenance of the family. At the present time he is paying $35 weekly. It seems Mr. Brown visited with his children for the last time about two and a half years ago. He told us he is interested in them, that he waves to them, but that Mrs. Brown has poisoned their minds against him. He doubts that the little girl even knows that he is her father. In the meanwhile, he has continued to live with his parents.

Economic Situation

Mr. Strine, Mrs. Brown's father, is a retired railroad man. He has a small pension which he shares with his daughter.

Mrs. Brown works as a dental assistant. At the present time she is averaging about $45 a week. Mr. Brown owns and operates Employment Services, Inc., and averages about $60 a week. He told us his parents have a little money, but that they are not going to give it to him.

Collateral Information

We have learned from various sources that early in 1959 Mr. Brown and a divorcee, the woman with whom he is in business, were in Florida and lived there as man and wife. Also, at the present time she has an apartment in the building where the present business is located. While Mr. Brown has not indicated to us his intentions as far as this woman is concerned, we get the impression that it has gone to the point where if he is divorced from Mrs. Brown he will probably marry her.

There is also a report to the effect that this woman has a son who is about the age of Mr. Brown's second child, Lee, who was born on April 23, 1949.

School

Mr. C. S. Detweiler, with whom we have had most of our dealings concerning Waln, told us that the boy failed the ninth grade last year and is repeating it again this year. It seems that the boy failed Algebra, Pennsylvania History and Art. At the present time he is getting the lowest possible mark in Pennsylvania History and in Science. He is also failing typing. However, the boy's earlier grades are sufficiently high to give him an over-all passing grade.

His attendance this year leaves very much to be desired. For example, in the first six weeks' marking period he was absent two days; the second, seven days; the third, ten and one-half days; the fourth, three days. As of this writing the school does not have a record of his last marking period attendance.

The school reports that Waln has an I.Q. of 110, which places him on the borderline of the superior grouping. Actually, he ought to be able to get A's and B's with very little effort.

During a recent visit with Waln he told us that the school works on his nerves. He would prefer to be outside and busy. He said he was having difficulty with Typing and History. He also told us about his poor work in Science. As of this date Waln has the attitude that school is hopeless.

Developmental History of Boy

We learned that Waln was the result of a full term pregnancy, with a forceps delivery. He was considered to be healthy, but extremely nervous and was a bedwetter until about nine years of age. The history indicates that he is an impatient, inconsiderate and ungovernable youngster.

Appearance of Boy

Waln is a tall youngster. We would say that he is nearly six feet in height and weighs approximately 148 pounds. His facial features are small but in good proportion. He has light-brown hair, hazel eyes and regular teeth that are in a good state of repair. He speaks in a somewhat jerky manner and in a low undertone. There is a certain self-assurance about the boy, some of which may be a coverup. At the present time he has acute acne.

Boy's History of Difficulties

Waln told us that at first he was happy in school and fairly happy at home. He said he had not seen his father in over two years, as he and his mother had broken up their home. Recently he has grown very unhappy over school, changed his subjects around and eventually flunked the ninth grade. He characterizes his academic program as being "pretty hopeless." He told us he liked to work on cars and thought he might be a skin diver.

In discussing his environment, he characterized it as being "too old." He said he gets in his grandparents' way. He told us they do not allow him to bring his boy friends into the house and everything he does seems to irritate them. The youngster indicated that his mother works very long hours and has very little time to spend at home. He told us his mother had suffered an emotional breakdown about three or four years ago and was a mental patient. In discussing his contacts with the outside world, he mentioned that he had run away from a police officer when he had been apprehended for engaging in serious Halloween pranks. He said he slept in a loft and was turned over to the police by a man who subsequently returned him to his mother. He thinks the only real violation of the law that he engaged in was his runaway from home on or about March 23, 1960, when he and James Hartman, age 15, took off and went to Maryland. He said they returned two days later when they overheard the Maryland police talking about them when they were in a restaurant. He also admits it was wrong to have assaulted Gerald Klein, a sixteen-year-old-youth, in the corridors of the school. He said he was suspended from school for this and that he had it coming to him.

We talked very briefly with Waln about his experiences at the Lutheran orphanage. He said his mother made these arrangements, that he was admitted on or about June 10, 1957, and was sent home on June 21, 1957. He told us he was very unhappy there and that his mother had had him discharged.

In discussing his extracurricular activities, Waln told us he likes swimming and horseback riding and that for a while he went to the Y.M.C.A. and participated in several swim meets. He gave us to understand that he was a superior swimmer, as his mother had done a great deal of swimming and at one time was Health Education Director at the Y.W.C.A. At this point in our visit we got the impression that his superiority was mostly in his mind, as he gave little evidence to indicate that he was a team-worker or would put much energy into training. Later we contacted Mr. Daniels and found that the "Y" had been unable to "reach" Waln, that they thought he had a little ability, but what the boy needed most was "a swift kick in the pants." They found that he lacked drive and good sportsmanship.

During a recent interview with Waln we advised him that the school authorities had indicated that they thought he was at the end of his rope and that he should not be allowed to attend public school as he was not a responsible individual. To our surprise Waln said, "I think probably they're right."

General Summary

Waln's father and mother have above average ability. His mother is an insistent, possessive and very dominating personality. Mr. Brown is a rather cool, calm and fairly collected individual. Of the two, he seemed the most sensible. Mrs. Brown is inclined to be flighty, easily disturbed and is emotionally unstable.

The environment that she has created for the children has
not been entirely of her own choosing, but has been forced
on her by economic circumstances. It is a broken home environment where the heads of the house are much too old
and too feeble for the young children. Mrs. Brown's working hours are such that she has little time to spend with the
children, and when she does devote a little time to them
her nerves are frayed to the point where she makes rash
judgements. As of the present time Mrs. Brown is an emotionally sick woman.

The trials and tribulations that Waln has gotten himself into
are not too abnormal, nor have they been of the seriously
antisocial kind. To our way of thinking, this environment
could have produced a much more seriously delinquent
youngster than we are currently dealing with. Actually,
Waln is and has been, during the most impressionable period of his life, a rejected, overdominated child, and at the
moment he is striking back at society. And we are using
these terms in their widest sense.

Recommendation

Waln has lacked an opportunity to associate with his father,
and this has created unconscious hostilities toward his environment, which likewise provided little in the way of opportunities to do things he is capable of doing. He has been
dominated by his mother and his present behavior is part of
his pattern of protesting this domination. His mother would
like to be a civic leader, but is forced by circumstances to
work and this irritates her. His father has let the boy down
completely. The present situation indicates the need for
boarding school placement. This might be deferred if Waln

would promise to return to school and really work and finish out the year. In the meantime, we would make plans for the boy to be seen at the York Mental Health Center. If placement is deferred we feel he should be placed on probation.

PROBATION RECORDS

02094
Waln Brown

4-14-60   *Hearing:* Waln, his mother and Mr. Detweiler, of the York Suburban High School, appeared before the Hon. George W. Arkins in Juvenile Court on Thursday afternoon, April 14. Since Judge Arkins had been provided with the complete probation investigation prior to the hearing, we limited our remarks to the nature of the boy's referral.

Mr. Detweiler told Judge Arkins that at the beginning of the school year they had difficulty with his attendance, as nineteen and a half days' absence were charged against Waln. He also said the boy was repeating the grade. He went on to say that Waln's work began to skid downward, and when he talked with the boy Waln told him he did not know how long he was going to be around. He said the boy had truanted from school after he had spoken with him and that recently he had been involved in some fighting. He said that when Waln had been seen by the school's guidance poeple he told them he was unhappy at home. Mr. Detweiler ventured the opinion that Waln needed continued guidance and supervision.

Mrs. Brown told Judge Arkins that Waln came from a broken home and that he suffered a lot because of it for the last four or five years. She told the Judge she had had Dr. Yale see the boy on a number of occasions.

Judge Arkins spoke in a very fatherly fashion with Waln. The latter told the Judge he had been doing poor work in school because his grandparents had told him he was going to be sent to White Hill. He said his grandparents yelled at him, that they are getting old, that when he comes home from school he goes to his room and watches television or changes his clothes and goes down to the vicinity of the local garage, where he and a group of about eight other kids work around motorcycles and motor bikes. He told the Judge he likes to swim, to work on cars, and that he thought about going into the Industrial Course at William Penn High School next year.

In an off-the-record conversation Judge Arkins told Waln that for the time being he was not going to make an order of commitment. For the record the Judge said he was satisfied that the circumstances under which Waln had been living were not normal and that he was not satisfied that Waln had done everything in his power to cope with them. At this point Waln said that when he went to Maryland he did not think he was coming back because he thought you could drive a car at fifteen in Maryland and that he could get work down there. The Judge then told Waln that his future pretty much depended upon himself. Judge Arkins adjudicated Waln a delinquent youth, and, for the time being, released him into the care and custody of his mother, on probation, with the understanding that the boy would be back in school, put forth some effort on his work and obey his mother. The Judge emphasized that he wanted Waln to make a serious effort to do the work at school and also told the boy he wanted him returned to court at the end of the present school year.

We saw Waln late in the afternoon of the 30th. He told us that one afternoon recently he left school because he didn't feel well knowing he had to make up a detention period. He claimed that he went home and laid down for a while, took a little aspirin, and then got up and walked around the community for awhile. He said that for this infraction Mr. Detweiler gave him two more hours of detention because he thought that he had lied to him. Waln said he still has about eight more hours of detention to make up.

During this visit Waln recited the Ten Commandments to us. He did very poorly and brought his Bible along for reference purposes.

During our conversation Waln told us that his grandparents have been treating him a whole lot better and he also thinks that his mother understands him a little better. Whether this was a real or imagined situation, we accepted it as being real because it was the way the boy felt about it. We doubt very much that there has been much change in the overall home situation.

As we talked we complimented Waln on the improvement that we noticed in his acne condition. The boy made no mention of having followed out our prescribed routine with Physicians and Surgeons Blue Soap and we did not press him. We got the impression that Waln was very restless, and that he was reporting to us because he had to. We accepted this hostility and endeavored to avoid placing blame on this boy at this time. We chose later to characterize his present predicament as being more situational. At the same time we gave Waln to understand that we did not approve of him walking out of school without first consulting with at least the nurse or one of the principals. He assured us that it would not happen again. As the boy was leaving he spoke to us about changing schools at the end of the year and being ready to report to the new school in September for the beginning of the school year.

May 1960   On the morning of the 7th Mrs. Brown telephoned that Waln was planning to come and see us later in the day. She told us that he had something on his mind.

Waln came to the office having been excused from school by Mr. Detweiler. He said that he had left school again on May 2 around 3:30 intending to come and report to us at the probation office. He said by the time he got going, however, it was too late. He told us that he had been "chucked out" of

the Civics class on May 6. It seems the teacher, Mr.
Martin, remarked that the class was behaving like a
lot of ants whereupon Waln said, "Ants are smart."
Someone else in the class muttered "shut up" and
Mr. Martin sent Waln to the office. For this he was
given two more hours of detention. In a dejected
fashion Waln said, "You know Mr. Lantz, I am going
to get chucked out of school." Apparently Waln
was testing us to see what our reaction would be.
We deliberately made no comment to the statement.

During the visit the boy told us that his mother had
arranged for him to see a skin specialist. He said
that Dr. Lehman gave him some lamp treatments
and other medications together with some pills, but
that none of them were doing him "any good." Prior
to this remark by the boy we had called Dr. Milton
Goldberg and had discussed with him the possibility of having Waln admitted to the hospital for
a diagnostic workup through the skin clinic which
meets Fridays at 10:00 A.M. Dr. Goldberg said that
there were no hospital beds available for this condition and that it could be handled adequately on
an out-patient basis. He also said that if the boy
came into the clinic there was a possibility that he
might be able to get the rather expensive antibiotic
medicine free since his mother was supporting the
family.

While Waln was waiting in the outer room, we
called Dr. Lehman and explained the family finances to him and he told us that his mother
hadn't made any mention of this and that she had

sent the boy in with a blank check. He told us that altogether his one visit had cost him approximately $20.

It seems that Waln has difficulty facing people, has difficulty in making a satisfactory life adjustment, is unclear as to just what he wants to do or where he wants to go. He is at this particular period in his adolescent development where he is very badly in need of encouragement and guidance.

Following the boy's visit to the office, we called Mr. Detweiler at school and explained the total situation to him outlining the fact that the boy's home atmosphere is so tense that it is having a detrimental effect on his acne. We told the principal that Waln and his younger brother, Lee, sleep in the same room with the mother, that the household is dominated by oldsters, that there is economic want, it is a broken home, and that unless the school can in some way get Waln to like the subject matter, at least to keep him interested until the end of the school year, there was a real possibility that we would lose this boy entirely. Mr. Detweiler pledged his cooperation.

On Saturday morning, the 14th, Mrs. Brown came to the office for the purpose of unburdening herself of some of the home pressures. She told us that Waln comes and goes as he pleases; he generally gets in about 10:00 P.M., but fails to account for his time. She said that he is threatening her to buy a car. He has also threatened to cut his face with a razor so that he would be put in a hospital. She claimed that in one month she had spent $60 for drugs for herself and the boy. She went on to relate that she had been seeing a doctor, Dr. Samuels, an internist, and Waln has seen Dr. Lehman. During this conversation she divulged that at one time she had cancer. She said she has to go for a check-up soon. We recommended that she inform us as to the results. We took this opportunity to help Mrs. Brown to understand that Waln was on the downgrade in his adolescence, that the home situation had cultivated some of the boy's hostility, that the absence of the father had much to do with his aggressiveness and attempt to dominate the household. We were not able to satisfactorily explain to her his inability or unwillingness to put more effort in his school work other than to point out to her that his general boisterousness around the school ground, in the classroom and among his companions, was to cover up a basic insecurity and his acute acne condition. We made it quite clear to Mrs. Brown that the tensions in the home had a tendency to aggravate the acne condition.

On the 16th Mrs. Brown telephoned that her doctor assured her that there was nothing to indicate malignancy.

Around 3:30 on the afternoon of the 18th Mrs. Brown telephoned in a hysterical fashion that Waln wanted to talk with us. She said "He walked out of school again today."

We spoke with Waln and he told us that he had had an appointment with the doctor and that the school authorities would not let him leave in time

so he walked out. We made arrangements to see
the boy the following morning at 8:30. Waln reported to the office and said that he had asked his
shop teacher for permission to leave class five minutes earlier so that he could go to the principal's
office to be excused in time to keep his appointment with Dr. Lehman. He claimed that the teacher
refused to let him go from class whereupon at the
end of the session he left school and went to the
doctor's office without reporting either to the principal's office or to the man in charge of the detention room. Waln produced a certificate from Dr.
Lehman showing that he had appointments for the
afternoons of the 17th and 18th at 3:45 P.M.

While Waln was in the office we called Mr. Detweiler and asked if we might have an appointment
with him. Later, we accompanied Waln to the principal's office. Before leaving, however, we reviewed
for Waln the importance of his changing some of
his attitudes toward his family and toward school.
We made it clear to the boy that he could not expect other people to accept his excuses for not
keeping in line. We tried to show him the importance of doing each day's work as it came along
and of accepting responsibility for his actions.

When we arrived at Mr. Detweiler's office, Waln
changed his story a little bit when faced by the
principal. We pointed this out to the boy and it is
our feeling that for the first time Waln felt a little
ashamed.

Mr. Detweiler revised the boy's detention schedule
downward and the new plan was agreeable to the

boy. Later, Mr. Detweiler gave Waln a new class admission slip.

Following our visit, we were in contact with Mr. Yeager, guidance counselor, and he told us that recently Waln had passed the preliminary test for admission to the industrial course. This means that if Waln passes all his present subjects, he will be able to matriculate.

June 1960   On the 1st we were notified that Waln had been accepted in the industrial course.

On the morning of the 2nd Waln and his mother came to the office around 10:00 A.M. The boy looked very glum. He said he had not gone to school because he had not been feeling well. He claimed that he had a headache on the 31st and on the 1st. He said that he couldn't keep his eyes open during class and on both of these days he stayed in bed all day. He claimed that he had no pain in his head when he layed down.

During this visit Waln indicated that his final examinations were to begin on June 6 and that school would be over on Friday, June 10. When we talked about the treatment given to him by Dr. Lehman, Waln in a very surly fashion retorted the medication the doctor had given him wasn't doing him any good.

Waln was offered summer employment on a farm. The boy turned it down, preferring to work on lawns and do odd jobs around the home. We got the impression that Waln wants to do pretty much as he pleases. This situation will have to be brought to the attention of the court.

Around 4:10 P.M. on the 8th Mrs. Brown telephoned in a hysterical fashion that Waln had run down the street and had threatened his mother by telling her that he would be glad if a car would run over him and also that he threatened to cut his face with a razor so that he would be hospitalized. We suggested that she go around the neighborhood and he be intercepted and returned home.

Subsequently she called us and advised us that he was nowhere to be seen. We then alerted the police and asked them to apprehend the boy. Still later in the evening Mrs. Brown telephoned that Waln was sound asleep on the back porch. She volunteered the information that perhaps he had taken dope.

We called Dr. Charles Tarbert and he readily agreed to make arrangements for Waln's admission to the emergency ward at the hospital as a preventive measure. He also told us that Dr. Lehman had conferred with him about the boy and that he had prescribed certain medication.

6-9-60   *Hospital Admission:* Around 10:00 P.M. Dr. Tarbert called us that Waln had been admitted and that when he and his mother had come into the emergency ward the admitting personnel had a difficult time with Mrs. Brown in that she was demanding a private room for the boy and three nurses. Dr. Tarbert said that he had prescribed certain sedatives and that he hoped they would be able to detain the boy as he was very surly at the time of admission.

Conference with Judge: We discussed very briefly with Judge Arkins the boy's referral to the hospital and also the possibility of having Waln committed to a juvenile institution where he might undergo a period of healthy outdoor exercise and at the same time develop a more wholesome attitude towards life and at the same time accept a little more responsibility for his own improvement.

Shortly after our conference with the Judge on the morning of the 10th Dr. Tarbert called us from the hospital that Waln was threatening to break out. Dr. Tarbert characterized the boy as being belligerent, emotionally disturbed, and antisocial.

We visited with the staff at the hospital on the evening of the 10th. Waln was so sedated that he did not recognize us. The following morning we again stopped by in an effort to be helpful. Waln was sprawled out on a mattress in the security room, was very surly and ugly. He refused to talk to anyone and was refusing his meals.

On the 12th Dr. Tarbert called us to advise that he felt it would be for the best interest of the boy to have him admitted to the State Hospital for a diagnostic workup and he was calling in Dr. Lehman to prepare the necessary admission papers. It was Dr. Tarbert's feeling that this boy was terribly disturbed, and at this time was a menace to himself and others.

7

The State Hospital

I trailed a hospital attendant through a maze of hallways, rooms and locked doors leading away from the outside deeper into the confines of the Harrisburg State Hospital. Each step brought me closer to the unknown world where I knew they locked away crazy people. I wanted to run, to make a mad dash for freedom, but my legs would not respond. I was too frightened.

We stopped at still another door. The attendant unlocked it and ushered me through. The door boomed shut behind me. We walked down another hallway into a large room where women wearing white mingled with gray-skinned men. A revolting smell smothered the room.

The attendant pointed to the door of a glass office and ordered me inside. I followed his command, entered the office, and stood before a nurse who was speaking into a telephone. She looked up and smiled. I tried to smile back, but could not manage it. She finished her conversation, then hung up the phone. The attendant handed her some papers and took his leave.

"Hello, Wailin. Is that how you pronounce your name?"

"No . . . Ah, just call me Wally," I offered, not wishing to explain the Scottish name that was my great-grandfather's on my father's side of the family. How I hated that name that people always butchered or made fun of. "Wally" had become the simplest way to deal with it.

The nurse told me to be seated. I lowered myself into a chair to face her. As she fooled with the papers given to her by the attendant, I peered through the glass. Two rooms and part of a hallway were visible. To the left was a room about twenty feet square. Pressed against the marred walls were pieces of old metal furniture with ripped and stained vinyl upholstery. Torn magazines, checkers, playing cards, cigarette butts, and other debris were strewn on the furniture and over the floor. Two men wearing nightgowns sat motionless on a couch, staring blankly ahead. A third man twitched uncontrollably in a chair while a nurse stood over him. Another man lay spread-legged, half-on and half-off a couch, a yellow puddle beneath him.

In front of me, pale men moved like zombies down the hallway past the office. They disappeared, then reappeared, moving mechanically in the opposite direction. One man was involved in an intense debate as he walked, though his partner in conversation remained unseen. Most plodded the hallway alone, their empty eyes trained forward, as if to deliberately avoid their fellow pedestrians.

To my rear, the ward's main lobby extended thirty or more feet in length and perhaps twenty feet in width. Nurses and attendants dressed in starched white mixed with dozens of men. In the far corner of the room a television projected cartoons at two bodies slumped into couches. A third viewer, squatted between the two couches, buried a finger knuckle-deep into his nostril. A group of people were huddled around a table where a card game was causing much excitement while two men beside them ended a checkers match by flinging the board across the room where it hit a man who was sprawled on the tile floor.

After reading the papers that had accompanied me, the nurse took me into the ward to introduce me around. I stayed close by her side, using her as protection from the strange-looking men. Our first stop was the group of card players. I stood out of their reach.

"Everybody say hello to Wally Brown," the nurse instructed.

A chorus of gestures and greetings signaled welcome. I could only nod in reply. A lump the size of a cue ball was wedged in my throat.

We turned toward the television viewers, who had shifted their gaze to me. I felt lightheaded and leaned against the couch for support.

"This is Smitty," announced the nurse as she patted the head of the man on the floor. "Smitty's been with us a long, long time and we love him very, very much."

Smitty made some sounds that weren't quite words and waved a limp hand at me. He was the one who had been digging for buried treasure up his nose. He looked like a little boy who had been put in an old dwarf's body. As he glanced at me, his toothless mouth gummed up and down, giving the impression that his nose and chin were doomed to collide.

"And this is Smitty's best friend, Billy."

A round-faced hulk of a man looked up, babbling like a baby.

"Billy and Smitty are best friends. They do everything together. The two of them have their own special world."

I could see what she meant. They looked like a pair of escaped circus clowns. As they babbled, gestured, and giggled back and forth, it seemed impossible to view them as human. Then it struck me. I might end up like them, a crazy person cut off from reality in a mental hospital for the rest of my life. I shuddered and turned away, forcing back tears as the nurse led me on through the ward into the hallway where a few men were still pacing. They did not seem to notice us as we weaved past them.

The hallway stretched the length of the ward. A series of arched doorways lined one wall. We went through one of the doorways into a large room filled with beds and nightstands. There were a dozen beds in the room, six to a side. One bed had no linens to hide its stained mattress. The nurse stopped at the naked bed and deposited on it sheets and pillow case taken from the nightstand beside it.

The odor of human waste filled the room. The smell seemed to rise from the mattresses. Mine was no exception. I tried not to breathe, but could not hold my breath forever. Each lungful of dead air was worse than the one before it. My stomach felt like it was being pinched. Warm spit filled my mouth. An uncontrolled cough sprayed spit through my lips.

After a shower and shampoo my clothes were taken and I was given a hospital gown and left to fend for myself. I anchored myself in a chair where I could see, and be seen by, the nurses and attendants going in and out of the glass office. I did not want to risk being caught in a dark corner by a maniac. A half-opened, barred window behind me offered the momentary relief of fresh air from the relentless stench. I hid behind the pages of a battered LIFE magazine.

A loud thud followed by a burst of high-pitched gibberish sounded and Smitty came running into the room pursued by a bald-headed fat man in a pair of yellow-stained undershorts.

"Ira! Ira! Ira!" the man taunted between deep belly laughs.

Smitty flailed at him like a windmill but his toothpick arms were no help. "Fugin' son-a-bitz, ya!" he screamed, knowing his voice was his only defense.

"Ira! Ira! Ira!"

"Fugin' son-a-bitz, ya!"

Smitty ran around and around the room, the taunting man right behind him. "Ira! Ira! Ira!"

A nurse and an attendant ran out of the office. Another attendant rounded the hallway. They parted Smitty and his tormentor and after a brief scuffle, the attendants dragged the fat man through the double doors separating the lobby from the security room. The nurse remained with Smitty, attempting to console him. He lay face-down, wailing and heaving himself against the floor like a child in a temper tantrum.

Smitty became quieter. He lay on his side, sobbing, the nurses kneeling beside him, stroking and patting his head. She had given him a shot.

When the two attendants returned, the nurse gave some instructions and they picked Smitty up, and headed through the double doors.

A heavy silence fell over the room. The onlookers moved off noiselessly, heads bowed in a mutual acceptance of futility, and I tucked myself into a tight ball and tried to escape into the pages of LIFE. A picture of some boys playing Little League baseball took me back to the summer team on which I had once played. I could feel the sting of ball meeting glove, hear the crack of a solid hit, remember the pride of a run scored, the feel of the sun's warmth on my dusty neck, and the taste of the cool sweetness of a grape snow cone at game's end. But, most of all, I remembered my friends and the freedom we shared during summer vacations. I wondered what they were doing and wished to be with them once more. Then I realized I was no longer part of their world.

The sound of a bell drew my attention to a line of patients parading mechanically into the lobby. When I started off the chair to find a place in the line being formed, an attendant shouted through the office window for me to stay seated until the group left. I did as he said and watched the rag-tag group leave with an attendant.

"You can come with us now, Wally," said an attendant busy gathering those of us who remained.

Five sickly men who stank of old age and piss were my companions. We moved down the hallway through several locked doors into a large room that contained a number of long tables. Seated around the tables were a bunch of old people draped in white gowns. Nearly a dozen attendants and nurses stood watchfully behind the seated patients. There was silence as we entered the room and were assigned seats. Blank faces stared into space. Pale and disheveled, the old people sat in a bleary-eyed stupor. There was no life left in their eyes.

The food was distributed to us: boiled potatoes, corn, a greasy piece of meat, bread, milk, and pineapple chunks. My stomach grumbled its emptiness. The first bite tasted as foul as the putrid smell that hung heavy in the room where old people who could no longer control their bodies farted and pissed at the tables.

The other patients approached their meals with varying interest. A few attacked their plates. Others toyed with or picked at their portions. Many had to be fed by the nurses and attendants. Few were overweight.

"What's the matter, Wally, aren't you hungry?" asked the attendant who escorted us.

I shook my head.

The old man to my left looked at me for the first time, gently patted my knee, then returned to his former position, staring silently ahead. His plate was untouched.

A man seated across the table eyeballed my plate. I shoved it toward him. His hands grabbed up the contents. He thrust his fingers onto the plate and into his mouth, forming a goatee of spit and unswallowed food.

I folded my arms on the table and burrowed my face into them, struggling for understanding: *I'm not crazy. I'm not crazy. I'm not crazy. Am I?*

8

In a Corner

As the time crawled by, there was little difference between one day and another. Each day was filled with fear, frustration, tension, uncertainty, helplessness and the dread of being forgotten behind locked doors and barred windows, cut off from the rest of life. Each day I prayed for release. Each night I went to sleep cursing the darkness and the failure of my prayers. Morning brought only a temporary reprieve from the nightmares—and another day to be endured.

At the end of the first week I was given the privilege of eating in the main cafeteria. It was a small but welcome relief. The food was better; the stink less. I was also assigned to an outside detail where I was expected to pull weeds. It was supposed to be part of my therapy. I lasted four days, then quit. Pulling weeds did not seem like a very good way to get at my problems.

Other forms of therapy were employed as well. Medication was considered the easiest way to control our behavior. Several times a day a line formed in front of the office and, one by one, tiny white cups containing colored pills were doled out to us. At first I swallowed them down, afraid to do otherwise. But when I connected the pills to the drowsy weakness that followed, I soon learned how to hide them between gums and cheek. They were not going to turn me into a zombie.

Insulin and electroshock were also part of the therapeutic program. Even as a naive fifteen-year-old, I questioned such impersonal treatment. There was no greater fear among the patients than the possibility of having your brain "fried." Shock treatments were a regular occurrence. I often imagined being led into that room, as I had seen others led—the room that smelled of pain, the room that jolted people into screams, the room you walked into but from which you were carried. Patients subjected to such treatment always returned looking expressionless, pale, feeble, and beaten.

Nobody took the time to explain to me that the program to which I had been assigned was primarily diagnostic rather than therapeutic. Not knowing that placement was for ninety days or less, I perceived it as potentially infinite. I might have responded more positively had such information been adequately imparted; instead, I spent most of the time fearing prolonged commitment and worrying about my sanity.

Several times each week, especially during the first month, an attendant escorted me through the labyrinth of underground tunnels that connected the buildings, and I was given chest x-rays, electroencephalograms, urinalyses, blood tests, and a host of others, including a battery of psychological tests. The constant probing and prodding made me both suspicious and fearful and I responded with minimal cooperation.

Another form of diagnosis was attempted under the guise of psychiatric counseling. Of the two doctors assigned my case, the first, Dr. Hooper, interviewed me no more than five times while the second, Dr. Walters, saw me even less. There was also a staff meeting where I was presented before a group of doctors. In all instances, I responded to their questions in a guarded and superficial manner. Not one of these "professionals" took the time to build even the slightest rapport or trust. Yet they expected me to answer their probing queries concerning my deepest, darkest, and most confusing problems as though we were old friends. I gave them a minimun of information. Who were they to inquire about my relationship with mother? I loved her and felt it necessary to protect us both. If they had approached me in a less mechanical, more sympathetic manner, I might have provided them deeper insights.

There were some staff people, however, to whom I did respond. The student nurses in candy-striped uniforms who visited on weekday afternoons did not pry, force, or analyze, offering instead, warmth, kindness, and sincerity. We played games, talked, or just sat together when there was nothing to say. When I felt the need, it was to them that I took my thoughts and concerns. There were also two night attendants—college students working to pay their tuition—who always had an extra cigarette or a kind word and often joined in on conversations, helping us feel a little less removed from the real world. I suppose the youth of the candy-stripers and night attendants may have had something to do with their openness and kindness. They had not yet been corrupted by time and professionalism.

In time I even made friends and acquaintanceships among some of the patients. A few seemed perfectly sane; victims who, like me, had been placed there for lack of a more appropriate approach.

The two boys on the ward with whom I found it easiest to identify had preceded my arrival by at least two months. It was with them that I became most involved, spending many hours sharing past experiences, present thoughts, and future concerns, each of us drawing strength from the other's support. Through them I learned the workings of the hospital and came to know who could be trusted among the staff and patients. Without their help and friendship I would have closed myself off even more than I did.

Tommy was thirteen. His short, chubby body, pale blue eyes, freckles, strawberry-blonde hair, and babyish smile gave him a very cuddly appearance. Everybody catered to him, especially the nurses. But it was to men that he was drawn. Wherever he went, whatever he did, he was in constant contact with a male patient or attendant. He would sit on laps, hold hands, or press himself against a leg, forever clinging to a favorite person in order to capture some semblance of recognition and love. His mother had died during his birth. The father was, according to Tommy, a "very important businessman" whose job kept him perpetually traveling. His son rarely saw him. Tommy had been passed among relatives and sent to a series of foster homes and a military school before being placed at the state hospital. Two attempted suicides were the cause of commitment: an overdose of sleeping pills that had been quickly pumped from his stomach, and a more adamant attempt at self-destruction that had left deep gashes across both wrists. Within a month of my arrival, Tommy left to live with an aunt and uncle.

Johnny, who was one month older than me, was almost pretty. Nearly six feet tall and of slender build, with brown hair and eyes and a flawless complexion, he was always neatly dressed. Only a chipped front tooth and two facial scars marred his good looks. It was with him that I formed the closest relationship. We smoked endless cigarettes while sharing many intimate details of our lives. Johnny's father had been killed in a car accident before his tenth birthday. They had been very close, like best friends. Johnny and his mother both had trouble handling the loss. His mother began drinking, her loneliness leading her through a series of men brought home from bars until she finally married one—a man who beat Johnny and sometimes smacked his mother. When Johnny fought back, the beatings grew more frequent and severe. Then, one day in school, a teacher tried to discipline him for acting up in class. Johnny rammed his head into the man's belly, taking his years of anguish out on the teacher. He was expelled from school, sent to a detention center, adjudicated a delinquent, and placed in the state hospital for diagnosis. He ran away six weeks after I arrived. He knew he could not go home and survive. They caught him in less than a day and sent him to a juvenile reformatory.

With Tommy and Johnny gone, there were few diversions to break the routine. A Friday afternoon crafts class of pot holder-making and gimp-weaving held little interest. Mr. Lantz once came in the middle of the week. We talked for awhile, then he left to confer with Dr. Walters. Nearly every Sunday someone from the family visited. We walked around the beautifully kept lawns while they pretended that all was right with the world. I never knew what to say, except to plead for release. The visits with mother were always strained. I blamed her for the predicament. More than once we parted company in tears: hers the result of my accusations, mine caused by the realization that she could leave and I could not. The next door neighbors brought Nanan for a visit. I cut it short. The shame of being considered crazy was not something I wished to expose to people who had formerly viewed me differently.

But most of all I sat alone or walked the hallway and counted the weeks, days, hours, and minutes of confinement. I saw a man lie down on the floor and die. Another man tried to hang himself, but was unsuccessful in his attempt at escape. Several others smashed their heads against the walls, then fell unconscious. Such scenes were regular occurrences. I drew deeper and deeper into myself, trying to keep my sanity.

I had a recurring dream. It was so clear I thought it had actually happened. I was standing in a corner when all of a sudden I began to shrink. I kept getting smaller and smaller and smaller until I became a little dot where the three lines of the corner met. All the time I was shrinking I was yelling for help. Nobody heard or noticed me. The smaller I got the weaker my voice was. I became so small that nobody could see me. It was as though I was not there, except I was. I could see myself, but nobody else could. I was just this little speck in the corner that nobody knew was there.

9

Psychiatric Assessment

For seventy-seven days and nights I was forced to live in the state hospital while the clinical staff evaluated my condition. The following comments taken from hospital records of tests and interviews conducted during my stay display the doctors' findings.

PSYCHOLOGICAL EXAMINATION
6–27–60

Tests

Wechsler-Bellevue Scale
  Verbal I.Q. 122
  Performance I.Q. 127
  Full Scale I.Q. 128

Bender Gestalt
Figure Drawings
Rorschach

Discussion

The patient was friendly and cooperative, but inclined to be rather nervous and restless, showing tension, quick, spontaneous responses, but poorly sustained attention. He has a severe case of acne and is somewhat self-conscious about this, mentioning it as one of his "problems."

The Wechsler-Bellevue tests show superior intelligence. A considerable degree of ego-intactness is maintained and the structured tests do not reveal impairment of conventional judgment, or show confusion of thinking or perceptual distortions. Social judgment is weak and somewhat fragmented. Concentrated effort and attention are variable. While the patient does well those tasks he can do easily and quickly, when interest flags, effort is not sustained. His range of information is narrow (considering his general level of intelligence), with occasional superficial and somewhat pretentious contributions.

The Bender Gestalt reveals no distortion in perception, but suggests weak drive and poorly integrated effort. The figure and other drawings point to a rather static and empty self concept, as well as instability of the sex role and ineffectuality traits.

The most significant features of the Rorschach findings are the narrow associational content, the variability and unpredictability in the use of energy, and flight and withdrawal of attention suggesting anxiety and tension. The patient seems unable to make up his mind whether to rebel against or to accept a passive role, to submit to unwelcome circumstances or to assert himself. His mental life is considerably constricted, showing a lag in emotional maturity and revealing tendencies to depression. Patient is failing to organize and plan meaningfully, and reveals a marked lack of central direction.

Summary

The total test results suggest inadequate personal and social adjustment in a boy of superior intelligence, with an unstable emotional pattern showing schizoid trends.

SUPPLEMENTAL CASE HISTORY
7–11–60

Abstract

On his admittance here he was well composed, cooperative and friendly, but quite guarded, and has continued that way without losing control of his emotions. He was seen in a number of interviews and it has been quite difficult to really reach him beyond a light social conversation. He creates a general feeling of detachment and coolness discussing his problems in school, in family life and at court. He is evasive in quite an efficient and not very conspicuous manner showing a tendency to belittle all his difficulties. He reiterates what is reported in the probation papers, that he is not too much interested in school. For instance, he thinks that not having a father is one of the main reasons for difficulties. He places a great deal of emphasis on his conviction that he has changed now and can live without getting in difficulties with his family and the authorities, and that he was just not able to see things right before he came to our hospital. However, it is quite obvious that he is not serious about those statements. He also concentrates on his acne and says this is another important cause for his insecurity since "people look at him in a peculiar way" on account of the skin condition. It is felt that his relationship to his mother is at a crucial point which is confirmed by his particularly strong resistance in giving information about this. He really does not say anything about his relationship to her but evades into lamentations about not having a father who takes care of him and his problems. Many times it is quite obvious that he judges things with his mother's eyes although he tries to omit this. There is no indication of definite delusions or hallucinations. The boy seems to be of superior intelligence, no memory impairment. It is felt that this boy severely lacks healthy identification. He is also extremely immature in his mother-relationship. His main defense at the present time is withdrawal although there is anxiety noted. Placement in a residential school and long-term outside psychotherapy would probably be the therapy of choice. Psychotherapy of the mother is necessary, too.

It is felt that this boy's psychotic potential is high, that his prognosis is guarded and that we might even deal with the insidious beginning of a malignant, chronic schizophrenic process.

CLINICAL NOTES
7–14–60

Discussion

Patient has exhibited a sample of his previous behavior in medicated form here in the hospital. He has been trying to manipulate his mother, his grandparents, nurses, etc. He has been very unsteady in his ambitions. He has asked for several jobs, wishing to be transferred to another one constantly which was finally not granted to him. He has been very unfaithful in his going to the weed pulling detail to which he was sent in order to have some sun. Constitutional component in combination with extremely unfavorable environment are responsible for the psychopathology. His mother has proven to be a very incompetent person. Her behavior during interviews in the hospital is inappropriate and indicates a moderately severe regression on her part although she intends to be friendly and cooperative. Her relationship to Waln appears to be still on the Oedipal level on Waln's part which, in my thinking, makes the prognosis very serious—especially as it appears that her conflicting structure has been of long standing and is quite fixed. I think that Waln should remain in the hospital for quite a long time; that he should receive group therapy and have a tutor to follow up on his school work. He should participate in many activities and should have, if possible, a well-structured schedule every day. He needs a great deal of attention as well as firmness and authority and the possibility to identify with a strong father figure.

STAFF NOTES
7–14–60

Discussion

Patient is here on a court commitment. Age: 15 years. He was always tense and restless and for the past several years he has been seen for psychotherapy privately and at the York Mental Health Center. He has become belligerent, uncooperative, destructive, threatening assault on others, and self-destructive. He has a moderately severe acne vulgaris over face, neck and shoulders.

Dr. Walters: Behavior pattern, immature in schizoid personality.

Dr. Harrison: Agree with diagnosis as suggested.

Dr. Patterson: Attempted suicide when eight years old. Severe facial acne vulgaris. Schizophrenic reaction, adolescent type, with a very poor prognosis.

Dr. Andrews: I agree with classification of schizoid personality and believe he will probably prove to be schizophrenic reaction. Should remain in hospital indefinitely and have intensive psychotherapy.

Dr. Easton: Age: 15. Has shown emotional problems since age six or seven. Recently a truant. Seen at court. Given probation but became depressed and neurotic. Finally became assaultive and threatened suicide. No real identification with either parent. Physical factors not helping in adjustment of basic schizoid personality. Needs psychotherapy to prevent development of full-blown schizophrenia.

Staff Opinion: Schizoid personality.

CLINICAL NOTES
8–15–60

Discussion

In the course of three weeks the undersigned has been in contact with the patient on a daily average of one-half hour and also has had several interviews and discussions with the Social Service Department and Mr. Lantz the probation officer regarding the present and future status of this patient. On one occasion Mr. Lantz visited with the patient in the presence of the doctor and at the time it was the impression of the undersigned that the probation officer was favorably impressed with the progress of the patient as relates to his insight and judgment. The patient shows his improvement in the following ways. He realizes that the lack of the father-mother relationship has left him with a lack of understanding of life's problems because he had only one view, that being those of his grandparents since they had taken him to raise. The training, in viewpoints of training, as regards his grandparents are the same as those that his mother had experienced, and therefore in like manner he has come to appreciate the fact that this training was not the best for him since he has seen in his mother many failings as regards to application of insight and judgment. On this point, in the presence of the mother and the patient and the doctor, the mother has admitted the observations of her son, Waln, to be true. This admission on the part of the mother was recognized by the patient as being one of the first mature expressions that he was aware of, in the sense of truth, over a long period of time. In contrast, the patient recognizes the father as being what he is and therefore will not change. Since no change can be expected, Waln can see and understand that his father's interest and advice to him in the future will be of little value. He recognizes that he alone can change his mind as regards his feelings and his understanding and cannot expect to accomplish a change of another person's actions, deeds or thoughts. It is his consistent desire to help in what way he may at home and at the same time not jeopardize his schooling in preparation for the future. He has assumed the stature of understanding what would approach a normal desire in this case and for that reason it is requested that with the permission of the court the patient be allowed a parole status to be returned to the home environment so that he may contribute to the family and in like manner accomplish further schooling beginning with the fall term. This move to parole this patient is made with the full understanding on his part that he will have problems that may not come to solution in his mind and for that reason he has been asked to share them with his mother who in like manner has shown improvement with combined psychotherapy with the patient. Should the occasion arise wherein the solution is not forthcoming and tensions mount in both, it is suggested that they keep in contact with Dr. Tarbert of York or visit with the undersigned in order that we might not have a recurrence of what has already happened. The patient states voluntarily that he feels that it will not recur and that he is smart enough to ask for help when he needs it. The undersigned is in full realization of the fact that the patient has a lack of experience in applying a new way of life and for that reason may be a true failure and thus slide from a schizoid personality into a full schizophrenic state; however, lacking the chance to personally experience stress situations with a new understanding, it is obvious that he will slide to the schizophrenic state with rapid motion. One cannot assume an air of confidence nor a feeling of the same understanding unless personal experience can prove the truth of a new conviction and demonstrate by further experience persistent congruence and faith in a new way of understanding.

STAFF NOTES
8–16–60

Discussion

This is a 15-year-old white boy, carrying the diagnosis of schizoid personality. He was admitted here under Section 326–328, to be returned to court, but there are no charges. Commitment was necessitated because he had been threatening suicide and a more or less constant truant. When seen here first, he was extremely immature and history revealed that he had shown emotional problems since the age of six or seven. The family situation is extremely unstable. The parents are separated and the mother herself is a highly emotional individual. Supportive psychotherapy has been directed toward this patient, with the result that he is a little less anxious and tense now, and seems to be showing more insight into his problems and the situation at home. The mother is again willing to assume responsibility, and it is felt that further hospitalization would not contribute much.

In Staff today he is in fair contact, still a little tense and apprehensive but nevertheless, much better than on previous occasions. It is questionable as to how much insight he really has and at times one gets the impression that he is actually schizophrenic at the moment. However, the secondary characteristics of schizophrenia are not present and we are faced with making an estimation of how much distortion in affect and thought processes there are.

Dr. Pontiac: At present he has a better understanding, good insight and judgment relative to his home problems—a great change in his attitude toward life. I approve his parole with the hope that he will be able to adjust better this time.

Dr. Walters: Cautiously recommend parole with court's permission.

Dr. Harrison: Patient was enuretic until age nine. Antagonistic and contrary. Acne vulgaris of face. Schizoid personality. Affect flattened. Autistic signs of repression noticeable. In Staff shows drilled upon superficial insight. No change felt since presentation for diagnostic staff. Prolonged psychiatric care appears to be of questionable value. Prognosis is guarded. Feel that patient will become schizophrenic. Parole approved.

Dr. Patterson: Severe facial acne. Deficient personality structure. Clinically a schizoid personality, dynamically, he is schizophrenic. Consider his prognosis very poor. In need of intensive psychotherapy. Approve his parole and consider parole arrangement satisfactory.

Dr. Loran: An immature schizoid boy, who lives with a very unstable mother. Situation is not good in any aspect. However, I see no objection to letting him have a trial visit at home since the probation officer is now in the case, providing certainly more of a stabilizing influence than was available before. I would permit parole with the court's approval.

Dr. Easton: Boy of 15 who became depressed over severe facial acne. A broken home and an emotionally unstable mother have contributed to his trouble. Has partially corrected his attitudes and will probably respond better to supervision at home. Parole approved.

Staff Opinion: Parole approved with the court's approval.

10

A Return to Sickness

A "welcome home" sign hung from the banister of the front porch announced my return from the state hospital. Hugs, kisses, and kind words from the family and a handful of neighbors gave me a sense of acceptance and affection—a fresh start. Everybody seemed genuinely pleased to have me home. My favorite meals were cooked, special privileges were accorded, no harsh words were exchanged, everything was tranquil and pleasant. Life was as I had always wished it could be. We were a family, at peace with one another.

Within a month after the "Welcome Home" sign had been torn down, we had once again returned to the old patterns. I was being yelled at for everything and anything: "Don't do this!" "Don't do that!" "Where are you going?" "Where have you been?" "Don't make so much noise!" "Go to your room!" "Don't talk back!" No matter where I turned, no matter what I said or did, it seemed to turn out wrong. Somebody was always irritated or upset with me.

The illnesses plaguing the adult members of the household made matters worse. Grandad's rapid weight loss had transformed him from a big man to a scarecrow. Mother frequently missed work and had to spend much of her time at home in bed, zonked out by the many prescribed drugs. On at least one occasion, she had to be hospitalized. Nanan's nerves were shot. Her heart problems grew increasingly worse with the additional stress. It was like living in a hospital. Some form of sickness ate away at each of us.

Sophomore year in high school proved to be no better than my previous educational experiences. I had been accepted into the industrial course at William Penn High School where I hoped to learn a trade. It should have been an ideal situation: two weeks of academic classes, then two weeks of machine shop. But I failed in both areas of the program. I was unable to conquer the workings of a metal lathe and fared no better with the academics. I was soon flunking every subject.

The acne had gotten even worse. I felt so ugly that I avoided looking in mirrors. Other students openly teased me. On one occasion I was seated in the gymnasium along with nearly one hundred other students listening to the instructions of a coach. Seated behind me, a black boy repeatedly sang the same line from the Coasters' hit song, "Poison Ivy": "Late at night while you're sleepin', poison ivy comes a creepin' around." Each time he sang that line, he pointed at me and laughed. Others copied him. I was totally humiliated. After class I beat him up, but I could not fight everybody who made me feel ill-at-ease. That was the last time I took gym class that year.

In mid-October I turned sixteen. With parental permission, I was legally old enough to quit school. Neither Mr. Lantz nor mother would allow it, though. They believed I "needed" an education. I felt otherwise. Rather than continuing on the path of scholastic and social failure, I hoped to find a job, buy a car, and give mother enough to help rent an apartment so that we could live on our own. My school attendance soon dropped off to a few days a week, then even less. Mother and I fought each morning before school as she tried to force me from the house. Our arguments were always the same in word and action. The following scene is typical.

"Waln, get out of bed this instant! Put on your clothes and get to school!"

"But, mom, I don't feel too good."

"And what's wrong with you this time?"

"I got a headache. I think I'm coming down with a cold or something."

"There's nothing wrong with you! You just don't want to go to school! Now get out of bed and get to school before I call Mr. Lantz and tell him you're trying to play hookey again!"

"No! I can't! I feel too sick!"

"Waln, you can't continue to do this. You've already missed too much school this year. You aren't sick. There's nothing wrong with you. If you keep going like this you'll flunk school again. I've talked to your principal. He said you're doing poorly in all your classes. He also told me that if your attendance and grades don't improve, you'll be asked to leave the industrial course. Now you don't want that to happen, do you?"

"I don't care. I don't see why I have to go to school anyway."

"Because you need an education! Because if you don't have a good education you'll never get a good job! Because without a good job you'll be nothing in this world! Now get out of that bed and put your clothes on!"

"No! I don't feel good! Leave me alone!"

"Let me feel your forehead. Aha! You feel perfectly fine."

At this point mother would thrust a thermometer under my tongue and stand above me, hands on hips, her right foot pounding out an impatient beat, while I concentrated on making the temperature rise to above normal. It never worked. Even so, I would keep insisting until she gave in.

"Waln, I can't take this any longer! You're driving me to an

early grave! Please don't do this to me! Please don't do this to yourself! Why can't you understand that you're only cheating yourself?
What am I going to do with you?"

"Let me stay home. I can't go to school today. Please. I really
don't feel good."

"And what about tomorrow, or the next day or the next time
you decide that you don't want to go to school?"

"I'll be alright tomorrow. I know I will. I promise. Let me stay
home today."

"You won't get miraculously better and go out after school is
over? And you won't cause any commotion for your grandparents
while I'm at work?"

"No. I promise. I'll stay right here in bed so that I'll feel better
tomorrow."

Such promises were seldom kept. As soon as school was over
for the day, I would announce my recovery, don my clothing, and
head out the door to meet the gang. Then, after an evening of pin-
balls, loafing, fighting, or joyriding in cars, I would drag home late
into the night and, the next morning, attempt to feign a relapse. But
after a while even I tired of that ploy. I just quit going. No matter
what anybody said or whatever punishment was held over my head,
I refused to go. Before long I was expelled by William Penn and
transferred back to the York Suburban School District. I never
showed for readmittance. There was no sense returning to a scene
of failure, nor, for that matter, to any school. Legally or not, I
had quit.

It was not long before the authorities became involved. Mr.
Detweiler called from the school to question my non-attendance.
Mr. Lantz also checked. Mother reported her concerns to them
both. It made no difference. School was out of the question.

When I did not return to school after Christmas break,

however, my noncompliance with the dictates of the law finally had to be corrected. A juvenile court hearing was convened. Judge Arkins held his comments to a minimum. The decision had already been made. Mr. Lantz escorted me to the County Detention Center, where I was once again placed in a chicken wire cage and held to await transfer to the Pennsylvania Junior Republic, a reformatory for delinquent boys, where I was to be institutionalized for an indefinite period of time.

11

Official Viewpoints

As I became more and more enmeshed in the child care system, a growing number of professionals had reason to monitor and record their perceptions of my activities. The following selected commentaries penned during the four-and-one-half month period between court commitments should help shed further light on what happened and why intervention was deemed necessary.

HARRISBURG STATE HOSPITAL
SUPPLEMENTAL CASE HISTORY
10–19–60

This date the undersigned received a call from Dr. Pleasant in York, Pa., stating that Waln Brown and his mother would not be able to keep their appointment this date for 1:30 P.M. The reason for the inability to keep the appointment is given as illness on the part of the mother for which she was hospitalized; however, the doctor reporting the inability was unable to give a diagnosis, let alone symptomatology as regards the reason for the patient's inability to meet the appointment. The appointment had been initiated at the request of Mr. Lantz, parole officer in Waln's case and for this reason the doctor relaying the message above was requested to contact Mr. Lantz in York and convey to him the same message as was given to the doctor. It is the opinion of the undersigned that this call to notify the undersigned of the inability of the patient and his mother to keep the appointment is purposeful and willfully done to avoid contact. The reason for such action is not quite clear, and for this reason Mr. Lantz was requested to be notified through Dr. Pleasant. It is understood from the history and confirmed by other factors in this case that Waln's mother has been working for several doctors in the area and currently has used several of them to cover up her mistakes and inadequacy. This appears to be a flagrant use of this mechanism again in her case. It is anticipated that should she continue this behavior, it will certainly produce in Waln a very unsavory mental attitude and may cause his deterioration and result in an acute schizophrenic reaction.

YORK COUNTY JUVENILE PROBATION OFFICE
PROBATION RECORD

September 1960   We visited with Waln's grandfather on the 13th. He told us that he thought the conditions in the home had quieted down, that Waln was ever so much better since he returned from Harrisburg and that he thought his mother seemed more relaxed.

Following our visit with Mr. Strine, we visited with Mr. and Mrs. Brown, Waln's paternal grandparents, and much to our surprise met Waln's father. The three of them advised that Mr. Brown had had a row with the woman who he had been in business with and that he was severing his connection with her and the business. There was a question of some financial responsibility for debts that the company had incurred. At the present time he is driving for the Yellow Cab Company. He gave us to understand that he had a "big deal" cooking.

We were very impressed with Mr. Brown's parents as they seemed to be fairly stable individuals, were concerned about the grandchildren and even their daughter-in-law. They told us that recently Mr. Brown had taken Mrs. Brown out to dinner. They said that they had hoped they might effect a reconciliation. We strongly encouraged this move as it was our feeling it would give a very real psychological boost to the children and especially Waln.

On the 28th we spoke with Mr. Burns who operates a local restaurant in an endeavor to procure a little part-time work for Waln. He agreed to interview the boy and we wrote Waln telling him to contact him.

October 1960 We had a visit from Waln's mother on the afternoon of the 13th. She was tense, on the verge of tears and so keyed up that we had great difficulty in getting her to the point where she could verbalize what had happened since Waln had come home. At one point in the interview she burst out with the remark that a few days after Waln got home he began to run with the old crowd, picked up some new associates that are poor companions and kept late hours, did not come home for meals, and on the days she was in the office Waln had refused to get up and attend school. She mumbled something about his coming to her office and demanding excessive amounts of spending money. She also told us she caught him playing the pinball machines.

In her presence we telephoned the home and spoke with Waln. He said he had a headache and had not gone to school. We suggested that he take a little medicine and report for his afternoon classes. Earlier we had been in touch with Dr. Lang, at the Harrisburg State Hospital, and had arranged for Waln and his mother to see Dr. Walters on Saturday afternoon. These arrangements were brought to Waln's attention and he agreed to go. He mumbled something about getting a license to drive a car. We told him that at the present time this permission was being withheld until we could see signs of stability.

We saw Waln on the afternoon of the 31st. He told us he was not able to keep his originally scheduled appointment at the Harrisburg State Hospital, as his mother could not arrange transportation. They rescheduled an appointment for the 20th and on the 19th his mother was readmitted to the York Hospital, as she had fainted at work. He told us they doped her up, kept her a few days and then returned her to the home. He said she returned to work on or about October 26 or 28.

We talked with Waln about the importance of keeping his appointment at the Hospital and at the same time inquired as to his contact with the restaurant. He told us that his mother and Dr. Pleasant eat at the restaurant and his mother advised him they were laying off rather than hiring help. Waln said he has answered a number of advertisements in the paper but none of them had materialized into a job. He said, "I want a job so I can make some money." He figured he ought to earn about $20 a week and that out of this he would probably give his mother $5. It is our impression that Waln is using every device possible to get a little money to buy an automobile. While he professes to care for his mother, we get the feeling that there is very little regard for her.

Waln's acne has again blown out in full bloom and his countenance might safely be classified as being ugly.

November 1960   *Contact with Family:* We called at the home on the 15th and spoke with Mrs. Brown's parents. They advised us that Mrs. Brown was in bed. They told us that she had been doctoring with Dr. Salter and Dr. James Smoker, a gynecologist at the York Hospital, and most recently with Dr. Thomas Henry, the family physician. They reported that she had a bad case of nerves, that she vomited, passed out at her job and had to be hospitalized. They told us they thought Waln was mostly to blame for her present condition. While we were visiting with Mr. and Mrs. Strine, Waln came downstairs and advised us he had notified the school he was staying home to take care of his mother, as his grandparents were not able to lift her. We told the boy he should return to school as soon as the condition cleared.

Contact with Dr. Henry: We had a long, confidential conversation with Dr. Henry, the substance of which was that Mrs. Brown was a very sick woman, and that he thought she needed a period of rest in a hospital. He said he was not prepared, however, to take any steps in that direction, as he knew she would "fight it tooth and nail." He said that at the present time he saw no real reason for Waln continuing at home more than the weekend, but readily admitted that someone needed to stay at home and take care of Mrs. Brown, as she was visibly ill, but that he thought it was mostly a psychosomatic situation.

Contact with School: We spoke with Mr. George Potter on the 17th. He told us Waln was doing absolutely nothing in school, was lazy, indifferent, and was setting a very bad example for the other members of his class. He indicated there was no point in the York Suburban School District paying his tuition at William Penn, as he was not going to do any work. It was agreed that we would see the boy as soon as his mother's illness eased a bit.

Visit with Waln: On the morning of the 23rd Waln came to the office after an appointment had been made by Mr. Stevens, head of the Industrial Arts Department. Waln told us he would like to quit school because money is needed in the house, that he would like some money for himself, that he does not like school too much, that he is not getting good marks and, if necessary, he thought he might take a correspondence school course. We were very much disappointed at this boy's attitude toward life and toward school. He apparently has been trying to play his mother against her parents

and is now trying to play her against the school, as
it is quite apparent to us that what this boy wants
is to get out of school, buy a car and "run around."

Visit with Mrs. Brown: Just as Waln was leaving the
office his mother came in. He passed her without
any sign of recognition. During the visit that followed she told us she has been so sick she hardly
knows which way to turn. She said, "I very much
regret the fact that I did not allow the Court to
place Waln at the Pennsylvania Junior Republic
when he was originally in court." She told us he
went to one of the local banks and badgered the
tellers to give him $67 which he said his younger
brother, Lee, had accumulated by way of savings
and which Lee supposedly told Waln he could
have. Mrs. Brown advised us that she told the bank
to make the check payable to her and to close out
the account. She said Waln has tormented her for a
car, claiming he has one all picked out. She also
said that recently he has been keeping late hours
and riding around in cars, that he does absolutely
no homework and is not the least bit interested in
school.

During this visit Mrs. Brown advised us that Waln's
father is contributing $35 a week toward the sup-
port of the children. We told Mrs. Brown that under no circumstances would we give our consent
to Waln leaving school at this time, that such permission would have to be granted by the Court,
and then only if and when Waln was able to find
employment that would be acceptable to the
Court.

December 1960

On the 14th Mr. Potter advised that he was thoroughly disgusted with Waln, as the boy had been habitually truanting from school and they were going to return him to the jurisdiction of the York Suburban School District, as Waln is a tuition student and they did not think it fair to accept money when Waln did not attend class.

On the morning of the 15th Mr. Detweiler telephoned that he had heard Waln was to report back to their school. We advised Mr. Detweiler that this had already been brought to our attention and that at the time of our last visit with Waln we had indicated that this was probably what would happen and that ultimately Waln would end up back in court and be committed. Mr. Detweiler was advised that this was what had originally been planned for the boy, and had not Mrs. Brown raised such a ruckus it was what would have happened to him.

Waln in Office: Around 1:50 P.M. on the 20th Waln stopped to visit with us. Owing to the fact that we were in Hanover, he was advised to come in the following day.

On the morning of the 21st Mr. Detweiler of the York Suburban School District telephoned that Waln had not reported to school. His contacts with the home indicated that the boy was lying around and just refused to report. The school district is responsible for this attendance and something needs to be done.

Contact with Mother: Late in the afternoon of the same day we telephoned Mrs. Brown. She exclaimed, "I'm so glad you called; I'm desperately in need of help with Waln!" She said, "I just can't get Waln to go to school and he needs an education so badly." We assured her that we were planning on having him seen by the Court at an early date and would see if it would be possible for the Court to work it in on the schedule which was set up for the 5th, at 3:00 P.M.

General Impressions: It is our feeling that more than a reasonable effort has been made by the court to help Waln ease some of the tensions at home and to arrange a fairly satisfactory school program. The resources of the community have been made available to the boy and to his mother, and it is our impression that Waln is rejecting them. We have also tried to get his father interested in him, and this has been unsuccessful. Therefore, it would appear that the only resource left is to remove Waln from his home and place him at the Pennsylvania Junior Republic, as he will not be seventeen until October, 1961. In the meantime, he must attend some kind of program, and this would be provided for him at the Republic. This program was originally planned for the boy early in 1960, and in all probability would have been carried through had his mother and counsel cooperated.

January 1961   *Follow-up Hearing:* Waln and his mother appeared before the Hon. George W. Arkins in Juvenile Court on Thursday afternoon, January 5th. The Court had been previously advised of the community's failure to reach this boy and of our feeling that Waln was now ready to accept placement.

Waln told Judge Arkins that he had been looking for a job—any kind of a job. He thought he might get work as a car washer. He said, "I don't like school." When the Judge spoke with Waln about his sleeping in until ten or eleven o'clock, Waln kind of reluctantly admitted to his behavior. Mrs. Brown had nothing to offer.

Judge Arkins deliberated for some time and then told Waln that the history indicated that there had been little success as far as probation was concerned; that Waln had shown little respect for authority and that at the present time the only resource available to the Court was an order of commitment. The Judge, thereupon, directed an order revoking Waln's probation and directed that he be committed to the Pennsylvania Junior Republic until further order of the court, and that following his hearing, he was to be returned to detention until placement could be arranged.

At this point in the proceedings Waln told Judge Arkins that he wanted to make a statement. He said that people like to make fun of him because of his acne condition. He also told the Judge that the family did not have enough money coming into the house. Judge Arkins sympathized with Waln on this point but advised him that he had not displayed much energy in securing employment. The Judge also directed that the Probation Department set up a hearing for Waln's father and mother so that the Judge might have an opportunity to discuss with Waln's father his present earnings to the end that he might contribute something to the care and maintenance of the boy while at the Republic.

Visit at Brown Home: We called at Waln's home on the morning of the 12th and spoke with Mr. and Mrs. Strine, Waln's mother's parents. Mrs. Strine was awaiting the arrival of her physician as she has been ailing quite badly of late. Mr. Strine seemed to be in good spirits. He told us that Mrs. Brown had visited Waln on the 11th and he had also paid a visit to the boy. He reported that he thought Waln was in good spirits. His only complaint was that this should have been done many months ago.

Visit with Boy at Detention: We spent some time with Waln reviewing the program at the Republic, what would be expected of him and, in general, what he could expect from the Republic. The youngster told us in no uncertain terms that he had this coming to him and that he was going to do what was asked of him.

JUVENILE COURT HEARING
HON. GEORGE W. ARKINS, PRESIDENT JUDGE
1–5–61

Henry Lantz called as a witness and duly sworn testified as follows:

"Judge Arkins, we are asking you to interest yourself in a 16-year-old boy, Waln Karl Brown, who has been habitually absent from school, he is not responding either to our treatment or to his mother's wishes. It is my feeling that the community has exhausted its resources on behalf of this boy. I would like Waln to talk with you about the situation this afternoon. We did help in getting Waln admitted to the special program at William Penn. At William Penn he did inferior work, almost next to nothing. The school was obliged to ask him to leave because they could not honestly accept the York Suburban tuition for a pupil that is doing nothing in school. This was the report given to me by Mr. Potter. The boy was then supposed to report back to York Suburban High School and he has not done this. Mr. Detweiler of York Suburban has tried to reach Waln and has been unsuccessful and messages have been left for him to contact the school and report there and Waln has not done it."

By the Court (To Waln)

Q. "Waln, what seems to be the problem with the school?"

A. "Why, I have been looking for a job."

Q. "But you were supposed to be going to school?"

A. "Yes, I know."

Q. "Why didn't you go?"

A. "I should have asked Mr. Lantz if I could look for a job, and I didn't, I went out myself."

Q. "Why didn't you work while you were in school?"

A. "I don't like school. That's why I have been looking for a job."

Q. "You had an opportunity while at William Penn to go to school for a two-week period and work in industry for a two-week period, so that you would have the opportunity to get some education and also to learn a trade so that you would be equipped to do something in the way of getting a job or performing once you got a job. What kind of job are you expecting to get?"

A. "Any job just about. I was going to look for a car wash."

Q. "Don't you realize you have to know how to do things before people are going to employ you?"

A. "Yes."

Q. "Well, that's the reason Mr. Lantz made these arrangements so you could take the Industrial Course at William Penn and learn how to do something so that people who are employing men would be able to find in you a man who knew how to do something. I am sure you were not looking for a job all the time you were not in school. These reports indicate you spent a good bit of your time in bed."

A. "Yes, until 11:30—around between 10:00 and 11:00, usually, then I would get up and eat lunch and then go out."

Q. "Well, it sounds to me like you were more lazy than anything else, Waln."

The Court: "The history of this case indicates, as Mr. Lantz has already said, little success in so far as probation is concerned. There seems to be no respect for authority on the part of Waln either for that of his mother or for the school authorities or even for the court. We feel that institutional care for the time is in order.

"We, therefore, enter this order.

"And now, to wit, January 5, 1961, on consideration of the information submitted to the court, the order of the court heretofore entered placing Waln on probation is hereby revoked and the order of the court now is that he be and is hereby committed to Pennsylvania Junior Republic until the further order of the court, he is to be detained at the Detention Center until transportation to the school can be arranged."

12

Welcome to Reform School

January 13, 1961, was a gray bitter-cold day. Snow and ice crunched under foot as I was led from the detention home and put in the rear seat of a car. Handcuffs bound my wrists. A metal screen separated me from the two policemen who had been given the duty of transporting me the two hundred and fifty miles to the Pennsylvania Junior Republic. Few words were exchanged. The cops were not pleased with their assignment. I was pondering the unknown perils of reform school. It was mid-afternoon when we drove between the brick pillars that defined the entrance to the PJR. The narrow macadam road wound past a number of old buildings. Double lines of boys marched past us, hunched against the chill winter wind. We drove halfway around a large oval, then stopped before a long white building marked "Administration." The two cops sandwiched me between them and headed through the double doors into the lobby of the building.

For the next hour I was moved from one office to the next and asked question after question. Then, when it seemed I had run out of answers, I was introduced to a man named Uncle John, the houseparent at the Inn Cottage and supervisor of the orientation detail, both of which I had been assigned to, and he escorted me back out the double doors of the building where nearly twenty boys stood waiting at attention. After placing me at the rear of the double column, he shouted some orders, and off we marched, moving among the buildings, picking up and letting off boys, getting physical examinations and hair cuts, taking tests, and requisitioning clothing.

It was nearly supper time when we marched into the cottage basement that was alive with a confusion of activities. Boys were everywhere: wrestling, smoking, talking, shouting, singing, or dancing to the sound of a radio that blared in the background. The noise slackened as soon as Uncle John was sighted. Though a short man who looked to be in his fifties, he had a bulldog build that demanded respect. His eyes darting among the faces of the basement occupants, he gestured to a tall, dark-haired boy, told him to find me a locker, then walked away as though I no longer existed. I stood awkwardly by, waiting for the boy's instructions. He motioned me to follow him, pointed to one of the open-faced wooden lockers that was empty; then he, too, left. Frightened, uncertain, I looked for a place to hide.

Before I could get the box of clothes given to me by the institution's tailor shop put away in the locker, the hazing started. Cigarettes were the first thing asked for or taken. Requests and demands to do laundry and other chores soon followed. Name-calling also began: crater-face, pimple-pusher, scurf, faggot. I was surrounded, engulfed in a circle of pushing, taunting, threatening boys. I wanted to cry, to strike out, to flee, but could only stand rigidly fixed to a spot, red-faced and confused, wishing it would stop. Suddenly the circle parted and two boys strolled through the crowd to where I stood. The others grew silent. I reached out a hand in a gesture of thanks for their help. They ignored it. Instead, they picked through my belongings, took what they wanted, then left, laughing, while the other boys looked on and grumbled. With little left worth taking, the crowd quickly dissolved. I took a seat on the long wooden bench that ran in front of the lockers and stared forlornly through moist eyes. Never before had I felt so humiliated, so defenseless. I wanted to die.

There was no time for self-pity. A "come and get it," followed by the thunder of hungry boys ascending stairs, announced the evening meal. I brought up the rear of the line. At the top of the stairs, I was turned back. Shoes were not allowed upstairs, only slippered and stocking feet. I rushed back, rummaged through the tailor-shop box, pulled on the striped slippers, and returned to the top of the stairs, which led to a dining room where more than fifty boys stood behind chairs at the small square tables. I grabbed a spot and followed the lead of the other boys who were staring toward Uncle John and his wife, Aunt Emma.

"Announcements!" barked Uncle John. The room went quiet. "The Inn basketball team plays Main Hall tonight at 7:15. Choir practice will be from 7:00 to 8:15 in the administration building. Sproul Hall has been canceled for the rest of the week. Hospital line: Daniels, Baxter, Smith, Harris and Yerkovitz. Smitty, you take the hospital line. Let's bow our heads."

"Our Father, who are in heaven . . ." the voices blended.

The prayer's end brought an explosion of noise. Tables and chairs slid along the floor, dishes and silverware collided, and unfinished conversations were renewed.

"Quiet!" boomed Uncle John.

The noise dropped to a dull roar.

Fifteen square tables filled the dining room. Three or four boys arranged themselves at each table. Boys wearing white streamed between the kitchen and the tables, bearing pitchers of milk, pots of soup, and loaves of bread. One boy served Uncle John's table, where meat and vegetables took priority over soup. Occasionally, Aunt Emma threw instructions at those who served. The two boys who had picked through my belongings and the tall boy who had shown me to the locker sat at the table nearest Uncle

John. Uncle John handed them the leftovers from his table. I ate very little.

We were dismissed from the meal. A mob of boys made a mad dash for the basement. I followed less enthusiastically.

The basement hummed with activity as I slunk down the stairs toward my locker. A tall blonde kid threw a left hook at the head of a smaller boy. The boy fell to the bench at his rear. I took a seat, lit my remaining cigarette, and pretended interest in my hands to help hide the fear.

No sooner had I finished the last puff of the cigarette than someone from upstairs yelled "shineline." A number of boys filtered through the crowd, picking boys and sending them upstairs. I was among the group selected.

Dozens of mock-skaters slid across the dining room floor, pieces of cloth under their slippered feet as they glided silently across the wooden planks, pivoting at the walls, then resuming their quiet skate. I stepped onto two rags and imitated the others. We slid back and forth across the room until the floor shone beneath our feet.

Again we were dismissed to the basement. I sat by the locker, quietly, trying to blend into the woodwork, while other boys fought and played. Some took their evening showers in the large cement stall that was open to full view. Others changed into pajamas and nightshirts. I found a nightshirt in the tailor-shop box and quickly threw it on, afraid to expose my pimply body to their mockery.

"Line up! Let's go! Put them cigarettes out and get in line!" commanded the tall, dark-haired boy as he and Uncle John entered the basement.

Boys stopped what they were doing and formed a line along the lockers. Uncle John and the tall boy moved along the line, counting noses.

"Forty-six," announced Uncle John.

"Forty-six," parroted the tall boy.

"Count's right," confirmed Uncle John. "Forty-six present, five on late hospital line, and one AWOL."

Uncle John scanned the line of boys. He said nothing but appeared to be singling out certain boys with his gaze. The basement was uncomfortably silent.

"There will be no disturbances like last night," scolded Uncle John. "Sex play will not be tolerated in this cottage. The floorwalkers have been instructed to give me the name of anybody who so much as farts out of tune. Now bow your heads for the Lord's Prayer."

"Our Father, who art in heaven . . ."

I shadowed the flock of gowns up the three flights of stairs that led to the bedrooms. The tall boy grabbed my arm and guided me toward a bunk. I crawled onto the top one and rolled beneath the covers. The lights were put to rest, but my mind was not.

I was awake most of the night, sleep coming only in the wee hours of the morning and then quickly put to flight by the demons of my dreams. Bedsheets torn apart by the night's turmoil were draped in disarray over the side of the bunk. I lay in a cold, shivering ball cursing the invasion of the January sun.

"Rise and shine!" a voice echoed from another room.

I rolled onto my side, turning away from the announcement of another day to be endured.

"Get up and shine!" demanded the voice again, closer.

Around me, bodies began to stir. Springs groaned, limbs stretched and mouths gave vent to yawns. Reluctantly, I dropped to the floor and made my bed in the military fashion displayed by the others. Some already trudged the wooden floor, shinerags beneath their listless feet. Like slow-motion robots they skated, as though clinging to a few cherished moments of tranquility. For ten minutes we slid squinty-eyed around the room until commanded to quit our efforts and prepare for breakfast.

Following the morning meal most of the boys flocked through

the basement door, heading for work details or school. Those of us on orientation remained behind. We were not yet allowed to do as the others. We awaited Uncle John's command.

"Get outside and form ranks!" barked Uncle John.

We filed through the door and made a double line.

"Attention!"

Bodies snapped rigid.

"Dress right, dress!"

Arms reached sideways to touch a neighbor's shoulder. Bodies rhythmically adjusted position.

"Eyes front!"

Falling hands slapped thighs. Heads snapped forward.

"Right face!"

Bodies quarter-turned with varying degrees of smartness. With each order, I attempted to copy the moves of those around me.

"Forward march! Your left. Your left. Your left, right, left. Keep in step, Brown."

The day was spent marching from one place to another, learning the layout of the campus. Nearly three hundred fifty boys inhabited seven cottages. A farm, tailor shop, chapel, guidance office, gymnasium, recreational building, shop, swimming pool, playing field, and a combination administration/school building rounded out the grounds.

Sometimes we worked at various group assignments: shoveling snow, performing farm tasks, picking up litter, cleaning buildings and rooms. Around such daily chores, boys were constantly being dropped off and picked up from scheduled events: hair cuts, counseling sessions, tests, medical appointments. But most of all we marched to the commands of Uncle John and learned to follow orders. On Saturday evenings there was a movie. Sunday mornings meant Church. Sunday afternoon and evening was unstructured, leaving us to fend for ourselves in the basement.

For twenty-eight days I was subjected to the same routine. Then, just as I was getting used to it, Uncle John called me to his room and informed that I was to be transferred to another cottage. Though I disliked orientation, and was fearful of many of the boys, I had made a few friends and did not wish to begin from scratch. My pleas to remain at the Inn were denied. Two days later, I left.

13

Initial Adjustments

Transfer from the Inn Cottage to Prasse Hall meant I had to master another daily schedule, make new friends, and manage to safely function within the cottage and on campus. The time had come for me to assume the status of "citizen" within the general institutional population.

In comparison to the old, three-story Inn Cottage, Prasse Hall was modern. It was a U-shaped, single-level, ranch-style building. The two wings of the "u" held our sleeping quarters: six bedrooms in each wing. The size of the bedrooms varied, several sleeping as many as fourteen, the smallest as few as four. Bunk beds were the only furnishings. We were not permitted in the rooms until 9:00 P.M., when we were expected to sleep. A tile hallway, bordered by unornamented wooden walls, ran the length of each wing.

The front of the cottage was wide and deep with a large kitchen in one corner, the houseparents' quarters in the other and a dining area between them with long picnic-style tables, a television set, and floors of dark green tile. Directly behind the dining area was a large locker-room. Long wooden benches fronted doorless wooden lockers across from an enclosed shower that bulged toward the doorway. To the right, against the wall, stood a large round washbasin flanked by mirrors. Further to the right rear were four porcelain toilets that left their users full exposed. A small room at the far end was used to store clothing and laundry. A mirror and two wooden benches occupied the space to the right of the door-way. It was here in the locker room that the bulk of cottage activi-ties took place.

Sixty-five boys varying in age from twelve to nineteen inhab-ited the cottage. All had been adjudicated delinquent and commit-ted by various courts throughout Pennsylvania, Ohio, and New Jer-sey. Individual charges ran the gamut, except for the more violent offenses such as armed robbery, rape, and murder. Some had spent the greatest part of their lives in conflict with the law. Many had been institutionalized more than once.

Charged with the responsibility of supervising sixty-five delin-quent boys were the houseparents, Aunt Emma and Uncle Warren. An older couple nearing their sixties, they were on duty twenty-four hours a day, with only one weekend off each month. Although they were dedicated, hardworking people, they were unable to constantly monitor and control all the actions of so many troubled boys.

On the first day in Prasse Hall, I was confronted by a situation similar to what had occurred on my introduction to the Inn Cot-tage. This time I was better prepared to handle it.

No sooner had I been assigned a locker and abandoned by Un-cle Warren than the hazing began. Several boys surrounded me, taunting, asking for favors, attempting to rifle through my belong-ings. One broad-shouldered boy was especially threatening. He de-manded that I give him cigarettes and called me "sweetheart." I stood my ground. For long seconds we stared unblinkingly at each other, our bodies rigid, ready to fight. His gaze dropped to the floor, then less confidently back to me. I put away my things with an air of pretended self-assuredness. The other boys dispersed. I had won my first battle for acceptance and respect within the cottage. Many more such tests would follow.

There were two boys from York County who also lived at

Prasse Hall: Darrell and Larry. Darrell was sixteen. He was at the Republic for the second time. His first commitment, for breaking and entering, had lasted sixteen months. Within four months of release he had been caught stealing cars, quickly recommitted, and had already served ten additional months. Larry was fifteen. A first-timer, he had already put in eleven months for forging checks. He acted tougher than he actually was. Perhaps his fake boldness was a way of masking his almost feminine good looks.

Darrell, Larry and I became fast friends. There was something comforting about being able to exchange stories about our common locale. They informed me that there were seven boys from York County spread among the other campus cottages. We all eventually became good friends. Each county had a certain camaraderie within the institution. It was a way of defining who could be counted on in times of need and a means of mutual protection and understanding.

Darrell and Larry and I became "partners," sharing our meager belongings and standing together against others who would attempt to bully or take from us. Our collective wealth was stored in a strongbox; cigarettes and candy were the most highly prized possessions and had to be guarded against theft. At the end of the month, when store cards had been used to the three dollar limit, even the locked strongboxes were only a temporary deterrent to skilled thieves.

The adjustment to a different cottage was accompanied by a new daily routine. I was no longer forced to march around the grounds each day. Instead, weekdays were schooldays. At the school, which was located in the administration building, attendance was compulsory for anyone under age sixteen. Some older boys who were too far behind in their education were given the option to work on campus. Almost everyone attended classes.

I was placed in the tenth grade. The classes were easier than those in public school. There was plenty of time to complete home-work. Most of the teachers were men, big men who doubled as coaches for the many intramural and extramural athletic activities which helped channel our energy. There were very few distur-bances in class. I soon excelled in all subjects.

On Saturdays I was assigned to a work detail. After working the first few weeks on the farm, I was granted the position of chaplain's assistant. Every Saturday from 8:00 A.M. until noon, I answered the phone and cleaned the basement office of the campus chaplain, Reverend Bland. It was easy duty and afforded plenty of time to write letters, read, and do homework. I chose that detail because I knew such a position would please mother, Nanan, and Mr. Lantz, all of whom believed that the religious life was the "good life"; I hoped it would display the evidence of growth that might lead to early release, but I also hoped it would give me something to grab onto, something that would change my life for the better. I was soon dubbed "Reverend Brown."

Much of my initial period at the Republic was centered around correspondence. I wrote letters to anyone and everyone, hoping for encouragement, seeking to keep in contact with the outside world. Letters helped ease the sense of being alienated. Through them I could relate hopes, concerns, and inner feelings that had no other form of expression. My effort to adjust to the new surround-ings may be most accurately represented by the following letters.

January 31, 1961

Dear Mom,

I just received a letter from you. I hope that you are feeling better by now.

I will probably be starting school soon, and I believe that I will get the job of being preacher's assistant.

You are not supposed to send stamps, for they supply them.

I believe that I know what my problems are now, but now I have to work them out.

They are:

1) I was not close enough to God.

2) I was worried about my skin.

3) I was worried about not having a father, and also about the family.

4) And I also did not obey, when I was told to do something.

I hope to clear these problems up, and thus become a better person, and also a better son.

Please write as often as possible. Also please tell me when you can come to visit, for I have much to talk to you about.

Remember always that I love you.

Your Loving Son,
Waln

February 8, 1961

Dear Mom,

I am now in the Chapel basement, helping Rev. Bland. I hope that everything is okay at home. And I hope that everyone is feeling okay.

I am getting used to things here. And I believe that I am getting pretty well adjusted.

This time I'm really going to try and learn. Before I just tried to get out. But this time I'm going to learn, and profit by this experience.

I believe that I will be home for Easter, which is a 5 day vacation. This will cost around $15.00 for a bus ticket and some money to spend on the way. Which you will have to send a little before Easter. Vacation will be from March 30 till April 3. Boy I can't wait till then.

Please write as often as possible for I love to hear from you.

Your Loving Son,
Waln

February 10, 1961

Dear Mother,

I received your letter marked Feb 2, tonight.

I realize that my behavior at home was bad, and I hope that I can change this. I am keeping a list of what I think my problems are. And I also realize that I did not set a goal for life. And that I should have taken more interest in school.

I took three tests today. In English Literature, where we are studying Julius Caesar, I received an 81%. In spelling I received a 92%. And in History I received an 81%.

I believe that I am pretty well situated now, my only worry is about Nanan and Grandad dying.

Remember always that I love you and hope you will visit soon.

Please write as often as possible. And tell me how Nanan and Grandad are.

Your Loving Son,
Waln

February 11, 1961

Dear Mother,

Today is Saturday and I am in the Chapel basement, helping Rev. Bland. He is a very nice man, and I hope to learn a lot about the Bible from him.

I must tell you what happened last night. Last night I was talking in my sleep, I kept my whole cottage awake. They said that I was talking about little green men??? One time I awoke to go to the bathroom, and a guy in another room gave out a yell like he was being scalped.

This afternoon we go to Chapel, and then tonight we will see a movie.

I finally realize that this is the best place for me. For if I had kept up the way I was going, I might have got into serious trouble.

I hope that Nanan and Grandad are okay. They have been like a substitute father to me, but I never realized this before. Please keep me tabbed on how they are. Don't forget, at the first sign of either of them being really ill, contact Mr. Lantz, and write me.

Well I guess that's all for now. Remember always that I love you. Please visit soon.

Your Loving Son,
Waln

P.S. Please send some pictures of the family.

14

The Social Order

The Pennsylvania Junior Republic (PJR) had a well-defined social system that extended from the top administrator to the lowliest boy on campus. Though the administration would never have officially recognized the full extent of the pecking order, which at the lower end had subterranean values, the residents quickly learned every nuance. This information was necessary for survival and gave structure to every action and encounter. By understanding the subtleties of the social order, and its various implied expectations, a resident could gain some control over the environment and establish his particular identity within it. Everyone had a relative position.

The institution was modeled after an extended family concept. Mr. Gladden, director of the PJR, was called "Pappy" to signify his paternal position. The staff members were addressed as either uncle or aunt. The teachers were referred to as Mrs., Mr., or Coach.

The administration was the highest order. They unquestionably had the most power and control, and were treated with special respect. Their decisions had the greatest impact on our individual destinies. Improper conduct in their presence could adversely influence release. When in the presence of an administrator, an otherwise foulmouthed troublemaker would display his finest social grace.

The staff was divided into several groups. Those people who wrote reports about our activities were the second highest order and were accorded courtesy because of what they might say about us; these were the counselors, chaplain, and houseparents. Other staff members who did not record or report our behavior were judged on their physical prowess, methods of punishment, or ability to relate, and treated accordingly. Some were shown false respect because they physically demanded it. Others were treated well because they earned it through their interpersonal relations skills. Those people who did not fit into this structure were always treated badly. They soon found employment elsewhere.

The teachers had a separate and distinct position. They were not employed by the PJR but, rather, assigned there by the Grove City School District. They had little direct involvement with the institutional administration and minimal influence on release. Their role was to instruct and keep us in line during school hours. Though they were excellent, dedicated teachers, the fact that the majority of us had a history of school-related problems made their job potentially difficult. Many students disliked school because of past negative experiences. Such problems were prone to create tension and lead to disturbances in the classroom. Their ability to perceive the reasons for such learning difficulties, coupled with their capacity to help each of us achieve a sense of success at something we had long failed at, made us consider them with respect and gratitude. But it did not hurt, however, that most of the teachers were strong male figures unintimidated by our aggressiveness. The men teachers generally fared better than the women.

While the administration, staff, and teachers held the top positions in the hierarchy, there were also boys within the general population who had special responsibilities and privileges that gave them status. These were the "citizens" who had been singled out by the adults as possessing qualities and capabilities that displayed approved forms of conduct. They were officially recognized and rewarded for their achievements.

The president of the student council had the most influence of any boy on campus with regard to helping the administration understand the ongoing needs and interests of the general population. Because of his ready accessibility to the top administrators, and the influence he wielded, he was held in high esteem by the adults and shown special respect by most of the boys. The individual cottage representatives to the student council were also highly regarded by the adults and by the majority of the boys in their specific cottage, for they translated group concerns to the president who, in turn, took them to the administration. Only boys who were perceived as cottage leaders were chosen as members of this elite group.

The night watchman had the greatest responsibility of any boy on campus. It was his duty to make certain all buildings were secured and to periodically check each cottage to see that nobody ran away. In case of a nighttime emergency, he was the one who alerted the proper authorities. He wore a time recorder and punched in at the various stops on his rounds. Because of the importance of maintaining order while the adults slept, only the most mature boys were selected for this position. The night watchman's privileges were nearly unlimited. He had the run of the campus, both day and night. Every boy coveted his position.

Another prized and highly respected position was that of the honor boys. Housed above one of the campus buildings in a small apartment called the honor cottage, these were generally boys who had been at the PJR for a long time, had exhibited good citizenship, and were planning to finish high school at the institution. They were permitted frequent trips to town, were less supervised, and had the run of the campus—liberties that stood in clear contrast to the highly regimented daily schedule most of us were expected to follow.

The boys who maintained good grades and could function properly in a noninstitutional setting were given the privilege of attending school downtown. Besides being allowed to leave the confines of the PJR every school day, these students received the best clothing supplied by the tailor shop and were allowed to participate in some extracurricular activities. More important they got to be with "normal" students, which meant being with girls—something that mattered a great deal to boys restricted to an almost exclusively male society.

As there was an officially recognized structure on campus, there was also an officially recognized social order within the cottage. The houseparents were, of course, the ultimate power; their job was to oversee and control our activities in the cottage. As the male authority figure, the uncle held the most clout, mediating over our conflicts, doling out punishment, and determining which of us merited special attention and privileges. He also functioned as an advisor with whom we could discuss male problems and concerns. The aunt served as a traditional mother figure, taking charge of the domestic tasks and providing a female perspective.

Of the others who had power in the cottage, the floorwalkers were at the top of the list. They were the uncle's ears, arms, and legs. At night they guarded us in shifts, reporting our numbers to the night watchman. During the day they kept order in the locker room and helped the uncle run the cottage. Floorwalkers were chosen for leadership, trustworthiness, and the respect they enjoyed among their peers. The better the floorwalker, the easier the uncle's job. They were expected to be obeyed and were given many privileges within the cottage. Every boy wanted to be a floorwalker.

The head kitchen boy was next in line. Chosen for the same reasons the uncle picked his floorwalkers, he helped the aunt juggle the meals, snacks, and cleanups for the entire cottage. The head kitchen boy told people what to do. Like the floorwalkers, he enjoyed respect, power, and special privileges. The six or seven other kitchen boys under him only had access to food supplies.

Two laundry boys shared the duty of organizing and distributing the clothing. Other than the floorwalkers, they were the only boys allowed in the laundry room where the bulk of our clothes were stored. Except for being exempted from other cottage duties, they received no special privileges.

The supervisor of the shineline made certain that all boys who had no other cottage responsibilities helped shine the floors. Each night after dinner he oversaw the distribution of shinerags and kept order among the shiners. Once a month he had the floor stripped of the old wax, rewaxed, and buffed to a bright lustre. His only privilege was to supervise.

There was also an unofficial social order on campus and in each cottage. Referred to as the "wheels," the highest members of this group held the most direct influence over the everyday safety of the rest of the boys on campus. They were the bad asses, the fighters, the ones who lived by their strength and guts. Everybody quickly learned who they were, one way or another. Even the adults gave them special treatment. They were ranked by their fighting ability and shown the kind of respect that is born of fear and uncertainty.

Each cottage was a miniature version of the unofficial social order. Each had its wheels. They were easy to spot. They had their own meal table, which was always filled with food. They never worried about second or third helpings. The best lockers were theirs— the ones furthest from the showers, where a wall could be used as a backrest. The bedrooms at the end of the hallways, where only four slept, belonged to them. They always had plenty of cigarettes, candy, freshly pressed clothes, and other luxuries. They slept late, stayed up after lights out, seldom got reported for misdeeds, and never shined. Among the boys, their word was a commandment. Where a floorwalker would report a boy for breaking a rule, a wheel would break a head. Even the houseparents treated the wheels differently from the rest of us. They knew that if they kept the wheels happy, their jobs would be easier. The wheels led a good life, as long as they stayed on top.

Then there were those boys who sought special privileges by brownnosing, "sucking ass" as we called it. "Suckies" were hated. They were the "rats," the "stoolies," the ones who kept the uncle informed about other people's activities. Sometimes they got a pat on the head or some small privilege for their reports. They also often ended up with a black eye.

The "flunkies" were the boys with little or no self-respect or confidence. In exchange for protection they did the bidding for the wheels and gave them cigarettes, candy, or whatever else they wanted. Usually the smaller, more frail boys, they followed every command and clung closely to their protectors.

On the lowest rung on the ladder were the "scurfs." They were the beggars, the ones who scrounged cigarette butts and ate food that had been on the floor, the ones who never changed their underwear or took showers, the objects used in sex play. Scurfs were treated like the plague.

Though there were some boys who never especially differentiated themselves with regard to any of the officially or unofficially recognized positions within the institutional social order, everyone knew of its existence and learned to operate within its boundaries. It directly affected each of us daily. In many ways, the avenues taken and plateaus reached within the institutional social order were indicators of how each of us might function in the larger society after release; for, like the larger society, the institutional social structure had the potential to inspire success or promote failure.

15

Hit Men and Heroes

Deviance was a part of everyday life at reform school. Somebody was always doing something that did not jibe with the rules. It was part of our individual personalities, a component of our collective identity, the reason we were there. We were bad. We knew that. We had been bad most of our lives, and had been told so—repeatedly. The extent of our badness was represented by where we had been put. Over three hundred of us who had exhibited behavior considered too difficult to be handled by the community had been thrown together. Instead of magically disappearing, our deviancies blended together to form a subculture that operated in contradiction to the rules and regulations of the institution. Its impact was less subtle, more direct, and we had to function and survive in it daily. The pressure from peers to be involved in nonconforming activities was unrelenting. Status and recognition within the delinquent subculture could be gained by proficiency at a prized form of deviance. It should be no surprise, then, that boys whose identities were so firmly enmeshed in deviance should continue their delinquent ways within the institutional setting and, also, that their values, norms, goals, and aspirations should be expressed in those behavior patterns.

Dominance, as defined by the ability to control situations through the use of physical aggressiveness, was the most admired quality within the institutional subculture. Fighting was something we all understood and valued. It had become part of our way of coping. Many of us had a long history of taking out our anger, hatred, and pain on others. Such physical encounters often had much to do with why we had been removed from the community and placed in a reformatory. Our physical aggressiveness had been perceived as potentially dangerous to society.

The institutional setting, with its large number of aggressive boys confined in tight quarters, served to encourage fighting. Fights were a daily occurrence. Somebody was always upset about something. The reason did not matter, only the result. A wrong word, a wrong look, or being at the wrong place at the wrong time, could create a confrontation. There was little to be done about it; either fight or be considered a "punk." Sometimes it was possible to find another way out, but not always. Usually it came down to a winner and a loser.

Fighting was more than a way to vent frustration. It was also a means of gaining status and self-respect. Most of us had never excelled at anything except, perhaps, fighting or other forms of deviance. Failure in "normative" areas of endeavor had led us to seek success and personal identification in ways that exhibited our feeling of being different. Recognition and approval by peers with a similar outlook helped validate our existence and domination through fighting offered the greatest reinforcement. To be considered a "bad ass" was the highest compliment and afforded the greatest respect. A "rep" meant power, and power meant control over people and situations. The top-ranked boys on campus and in a cottage had the fewest hassles. Other boys usually left them alone, choosing boys of lower rank on whom to take out their frustrations. Nobody wanted to lose a fight; it was bad for reputation and rank. Nonetheless, the time inevitably came when a face-off with a boy of similar or higher rank could no longer be avoided. It was then that rankings often changed and the power that accompanied rank sometimes shifted.

Not all fighting was done in the locker room or out-of-the-way places, however. Once a year there were intercottage boxing matches. Boys trained for months in order to win or last the three two-minute rounds that could help or harm their rep. The finals were always a big event. Everybody attended. It was an easy way to size up boys who might someday be adversaries.

There was also another legal way to fight. Boys could settle their differences by enlisting the approval of a coach who would supervise the fights. The use of sixteen-ounce gloves made it difficult to badly hurt one another, but it did allow the combatants to air their differences. The locker room, no-holds-barred style fight often resulted in injuries while the supervised boxing matches usually ended with two tired but unmarked boys.

Though winning a fight was most important, losing could be done without serious damage to rep. "Heart" or "guts"—the refusal to back down from any adversary or any predicament even when loss was inevitable—was highly prized. Some boys would get up a dozen times after being knocked down and continue to swing. It was the "punks," the "quitters," the "chicken shits," the boys who would not fight back who were despised, picked on, and mistreated. The "bad asses" and "hearts" were admired. They won their acceptance by dominating situations that others feared to face. They were symbols of our will to overcome.

Some boys took advantage of fear. They sold protection to the weaklings. Cigarettes, candy, money, sex, or other favors were accepted as payment. The safety they provided was usually not security against others but, rather, an assurance that they would not harm the buyer. Those who paid for defense quickly became flunkies. They were the ones who would never make it anywhere.

But our deviancies were not merely limited to physical aggression. There were other ways to pursue a delinquent life-style, other predicaments to exploit. Loansharking was one such situation. A three-dollar storecard seldom lasted a full month. Although some boys had regular visits and received packages from home to help refill their supply of cigarettes, candy, and other consumables, most of us had to rely on our storecards or wits for provisions. The end of the month was a time when demand was high and supplies were low. When somebody lit a cigarette, a dozen boys would beg "shorts" for the butt. It was a time when those who still had supplies could make a profit by loaning at whatever was the going rate. At the beginning of the month, debts had to be paid immediately and in full. Some boys acquired wealth, power, and status through the proficient manipulation of this business practice. Others fell increasingly deeper into debt. There were those who took and those who were taken.

Gambling was another way in which goods and services were exchanged. We were not allowed to play traditional games of chance since it was realized that the factors of luck, skill or cheating could be used for illegitimate purposes that might result in fights. We learned to circumvent such restrictions. Sugar cubes numbered in ink were an innovative replacement for dice and could be swallowed upon detection. Playing cards were made from small pieces of paper and coded. But the game that we were allowed to play, the one that was the major focus of gambling, was jacks. There were some boys so accomplished at this seemingly innocent child's game that they were able to win consistently and almost at will. They would "sucker" an unsuspecting boy into a game by losing at first, then slowly, methodically, part him from his belongings. There was always some sheep to be sheared, someone who needed to confront the odds and redeem or prove his identity. Pride was often both an asset and a liability.

There was also a word game we sometimes engaged in that we

called the "dozens." No apparatus was needed, only a quick wit and a long temper. Pride, not goods, was at stake. The game involved two players and a series of ritualized insults. The insults centered on the opposing player's family, generally his mother. The objective was to top the other player's remarks by making an inflammatory allusion that was usually obscene but witty and so derogatory and denigrating that it could not be bettered. Other boys would "signify" their approval or disapproval of each retort. The following examples are offered:

"You'll never be the man your mother was."
"I heard your mother had all her babies born dead."
"If you had a mother, I had her first."
"I don't call you son because you shine. I call you son because you are mine."
"I don't call you son for a joke. I call you son because I was there when you mother's cherry was broke."

There was an endless number of such insults. It was a game played mostly by the younger boys and often ended in a fight when one player's pride was too badly stung or he felt the need to defend his mother's honor.

Some boys chose to deliver insults in a less direct manner. There is no truth to the statement about "honor among thieves." Every cottage had its thieves. They were the reason we stored our prized possessions in strongboxes, or lost them. Even the best strongboxes and locks were not totally safe from the more skilled thieves, the ones who had learned to pick, jimmy, or otherwise enter without the use of the proper key or combination. Their presence was most pronounced near the end of the month. They seldom were discovered, so adept were they at their trade. Those who were caught, however, usually did not make the same mistake. We had our own form of behavior modification.

"Escapism" was also practiced. Running away was the most direct avenue of escape, and many boys tried it, but the low rate of success and the accompanying punishment limited the practice. Some discovered alternatives, though drugs were not yet prevalent and traditional forms of alcohol were nearly impossible to obtain. Cologne and after-shave contained alcohol. More than one boy professed to be an "Aqua Velva man." Glue sniffing provided a high. The rich or well-connected drank rubbing alcohol pirated from the campus dispensary. A few boys who worked on the farm brewed and sold "home brew." The kitchen boys had access to a constant supply of vanilla extract. Some even managed to smuggle in candies with rum centers. Anything was used that might keep the mind off the ticking of the clock. Time passed unbearably slowly.

To help fill the hours, days, weeks, months, and sometimes years spent awaiting release, many tales of past experiences and future goals were exchanged. Such stories often centered around the delinquent way of life. Stories of fights, gang wars, burglaries, and other forms of deviance were related. Very few of us aspired to become teachers, doctors, lawyers, or to assume other "legit" occupations. Most voiced the desire to become a Mafia hit man or some other underworld figure. Such aspirations had much to do with our self-concepts. We had grown so used to being considered bad that that was how we perceived ourselves. At least we could succeed at something by being the baddest of the bad. No one identified with the cops; only the robbers received our praises. The bad guys were our heroes.

An example of our fondness for the man who stood in opposition to law and order was well illustrated by the following toast that I learned at the PJR. The hero was the metaphorical embodiment of the value system with which we had come to identify. His adventures were our dreams.

STAGOLEE

"In 1932,
When times were hard and blue,
I had a sawed-off shotgun,
A cold deck of cards,
Three-button rolled suit,
Snap-down hat,
'32 Ford,
No payments on that.
Had me a wife,
Brave and bold,
Threw my ass out in the cold.
Went downtown,
Picked up a whore,
Went selling pussy
From door to door.
Went down Vampire Street.
Vampire Street,
That's where all the bad motherfuckers meet.
Waded through six inches of shit,
Twelve inches of mud,
'Til I came to the corner bar
Called the Bucket of Blood.
I said, 'Bartender
Gimme something to eat.'
He gave me a bloody glass of water
And a fucked-up piece of meat.
I said, 'Bartender
I don't think you know who I am.'
He said, 'Frankly, son,
I don't give a damn.'
I said, 'Stagolee,

Stagolee's the name.'
He said, 'Stagolee,
I've heard of your ways,
And I kill cocksuckers
Like you every day.'
I gave him a chance to say no more.
Six clicks were heard.
Six bullets in that motherfucker's head
And I knew he was dead.
Just then a bitch came running up to the bar.
She said, 'Bartender, bartender please!'
I said, 'Easy, bitch,
He's behind the counter with his mind at ease.'
She said, 'Stagolee,
You better not be around,
When Billy Lyons
Brings his bad ass to town.'
I said, 'Look, bitch,
I've been in the future,
I've been in the past,
And you can cram Billy Lyons
Up your motherfucking ass.'
Saw a bitch
Across the way,
Thought I'd go over
And maybe stay.
I said, 'Look, bitch,
I don't wanna sound silly,
But who's this motherfucker
They call Billy?'
She pulled out a square.
He seemed to be nowhere.
Sort of tall, dark, and neat.

Supposed to be the meanest motherfucker
Who ever walked the street.
Saw a bitch
Across the aisle,
Thought I'd go over
And bullshit a while.
She opened her purse,
Pulled out a dime,
And said, 'Stagolee,
Looks like you ain't had a good piece
In a helluva long time.'
Went up to her apartment.
Fucked her on the couch.
Fucked her on the floor.
Best piece of ass
I ever had before.
I said, 'Bitch,
You look good enough to eat.'
She said, 'Drop to your knees.'
So I dropped to my knees,
Like a natural man.
That's when I found out
She had a .45 in her hand.
She hit me over the head,
Threw me out in the alley
And left me for dead.
Out in the alley,
That's where I met Sally.
She invited me to the party of freaks.
Frankenstein was there
With a bunch of other creeps.
Frankenstein grabbed himself a bitch
With the seven-year itch,

Crabs up her ass so fine
You'd swear it was daylight savings time.
There was shit on the ceiling
And come on the floor.
That's when Billy Lyons
Walked through the door.
He went one-to-one
'Til he came to me.
He said, 'And who may this
Bad motherfucker be?'
I said, 'Stagolee.'
He said, 'Stagolee,
You dug your ditch
When you fucked my bitch!'
I said, 'Look, Billy,
I'll give you just one chance to run
Before I draw my gatling gun.'
Someone yelled, 'Call the law!'
But that was too late,
I had already punched him in the jaw.
Someone screamed, 'Turn out the lights!'
But that was too late,
I already had him in my sights.
When the lights came on
They did their best
To count 99 bullets
In that motherfucker's chest.
Just then the law came through the door
They took me out on a two-by-four.
The Judge said, 'What may your sentence be,
Self-defense,
Or murder in the first degree?'
One bitch stood up and said,

'Give him gas!'
Another screamed,
'Shoot electricity up his ass!'
A third bitch stood up and said,
'Sit down, whores.
You don't know what it's all about.'
Well, the Judge gave me twenty.
Twenty, hell, that ain't no time!
I've got a brother in Sing Sing
Serving 99. He's fine.
When I got out,
I changed my name to Dangerous Dan.
Supposed to be the meanest, baddest,
Roughest motherfucker
Who ever walked the land.
Too proud to sleep in beds.
Rode in box cars and shit lead.
I wrestled with lightning
And fought with thunder.
When I walked across a graveyard,
Even dead people wondered. Amen."

16

Spare the Rod and Spoil the Child

A lack of discipline had much to do with why most of us were in a reformatory. This does not mean that we had not experienced various types of punishment intended to "teach us a lesson" but, rather, that such forms of behavior modification were often ill-defined, inappropriate, or inconsistent. Some boys had received such harsh treatment from their families and other authority figures— regardless of whether their actions were bad or good—that they had difficulty differentiating right from wrong. Others had been given so little attention within and outside the home that they had been left to live by their own devices and standards. But most of us were somewhere between these two extremes. We knew the basic rules within which society expected us to function. That was not our problem. We needed a reason to adopt and maintain a more socially-approved way of life. To do this, we would have to gain insight into the causes of past patterns of behavior, and understand why such behavior was incorrect; to learn the boundaries for appropriate living, and develop new standards of conduct while attaining "legitimate" successes that could be translated to purposeful goals in the outside world; and, finally, we would have to learn self-discipline. It was a lot to ask of boys who had spent the major portion of their lives clinging to delinquency for survival. Nonetheless, this was the task charged to the PJR and to each of us.

The institutional rules for conduct were strict and well-defined. The month spent on orientation taught us to keep in step or suffer the consequences. Indeed, the militaristic approach emphasized conformity by restricting independent actions. Marching did not end with orientation. Even as "citizens," we were expected to form ranks when we moved in groups around the campus. When individuals went from one place to another they had to carry a pass authorized by an adult. Only the honor boys and the night watchman were allowed to move freely.

There were no high fences, walls, or guards to keep us from running away. A main road that ran through the countryside surrounding Grove City was only a short distance from several of the cottages. It was a tempting route of escape. Many boys tried. Very few, if any, made it. Those who were caught served as examples, for the consequences were swift and extreme. Runaways were subjected to physical abuse and humiliation. Upon return to the institution, they were paddled by the uncles. "Cracks," as we called paddling, were given by the biggest, strongest men. The paddles were generally three feet long, four inches wide, one inch thick, and made of oak. Thirty to forty cracks were administered. Sometimes pants were left on; sometimes not. The bruises and scabs could last a month. Runaways seldom sat for at least three days. A few of the uncles slapped or punched. Name-calling was part of the ritual. Then the runaways were taken to the barbershop where Gino, a former inmate who liked his job, gave them a "peeled head." Every hair was stripped from the scalp. "Knuckleheads" were also given. A lumpy skull symbolized the runaways' unenviable status. We were not allowed to talk to them. For the next thirty days, they had to work on the farm and do the rottenest chores on campus. Any and all privileges were denied. Street clothes were replaced by institutional work uniforms. When they were in the cottage, all their clothing was locked away in the laundry room, and only a nightgown could be worn. Runaways shined the floors from the moment they returned from "hard labor" until bedtime. There was also some hitting and name-calling from the other boys, part of the price for such a mistake. Like sex offenders, runaways were given "the treatment."

In cases of theft, fighting, or repeated minor indiscretions, boys were placed "on report"—a scaled-down version of the abovementioned form of punishment. Disciplinary measures were determined according to the administration's perception of the seriousness of the situation. So many hours of hard labor, a specific number of cracks, and loss of certain privileges were the usual penalties.

"Cracks" was the most common form of physical punishment, and was practiced by administrators, teachers, uncles, and other staff members. Every adult had a paddle. Every boy felt the sting at least once during his stay. In the cottage, where the paddle ruled supreme, the giving of cracks was a ritualized, nearly nightly, ceremony that was generally observed by the entire cottage. The victim was told to bend over and grab his ankles or a bench before the uncle whacked him a previously stated number of times. In many cases, this event was a contest between man and boy. The uncle tried to inflict pain. The boy attempted to hide it. Some uncles took a running start or hit low on the legs, seeking to bring the boy to his knees. There were some boys who could take the uncle's best shots without so much as blinking. These were the "hard asses" and were shown respect for their stoic denial. The ones who cried or crumbled were shown no pity. The ability to absorb pain was something we all knew and admired. It had long been part of our lives. The way a boy took it was a means of measuring him—and the adult who gave it.

There were some men on campus who seemed to enjoy exercising punitive measures. They tried their best to inflict pain. Some drilled small holes in their paddles or wrapped rubber bands around them for added sting. Still others slapped or punched their victims, displaying their dominance over those who, if they hit back, could be sent to jail or further beaten. Several uncles even had "goon squads" they allowed to beat up certain boys they felt needed to be "straightened out."

Though the threat of physical punishment certainly weighed heavy on our minds, and in many cases acted as a deterrent, I did not believe then, nor am I convinced now, that fear had a long-range effect upon us, except as a further display of human cruelty. A paddling is one thing; the intent to do bodily injury is another. We certainly needed discipline, but we did not deserve cruel and unusual punishment. Trying to manage the actions of over three-hundred aggressive delinquents must have been a monumental task, of course. Yet there are other less severe and more enduring ways to do it. Control is gained and maintained by healthy respect for people and their rules, not the fear of consequences. We had already proven that point by following our deviant paths beyond many threats of punishment. A different approach was necessary if prolonged change was to come about.

The institution also practiced some nonviolent measures that produced a more subtle impact. Shineline was one such form of disciplining. While a stoic response to paddling could be used to show heart, there was no way shining could be turned to an advantage. It was boring, time-consuming, and embarrassing. While cottage mates pursued other activities, a shiner could only count the minutes until allowed to cease the monotonous sliding back and forth across the floors. Wheels were momentarily reduced to the station of the lowliest scurf. Everybody hated to shine.

Loss of privileges took its toll as well. In an environment where even the most ordinary liberties were limited, the removal of one or several pleasures was a blow. For instance, the institutional economy was so meager that taking away all or part of a storecard created a predicament by restricting ready access to cigarettes, candy, and other consumables. Being denied participation in certain campus activities, as well as in formerly earned off-campus events, proved the same point. Since these approaches were more in line with forms of discipline exercised by authority figures in the outside world, they could be effectively related to situations we would encounter after release.

Even hard labor had its place, particularly when boys did not respond to the less direct disciplinary measures and had to be subjected to more rigorous penalties in order to learn the potential consequences of inappropriate behavior. Slopping hogs, cleaning animal stalls, collecting garbage, and other forms of unpleasant work offered a nonviolent example of how the breaking of rules could result in disagreeable, but justifiable, experiences. A few days of sweaty, smelly, back-breaking hard labor made a more lasting impression than did the sting of a paddle or the back of a hand. There was no glory to be gained, nor did it feed long-standing delusions of being misunderstood or maltreated by adults.

Yet what most greatly influenced my behavior, and that of others as well, were not the punitive measures but, rather, the techniques used to establish and reinforce socially-approved accomplishments. Many of us had adopted a delinquent way of life because we were unable to succeed or gain recognition at anything else. As long as that basic lack went unaltered, there was no incentive to experiment with or strive toward a life-style that had already proven our downfall. It was easier to maintain a delinquent attitude.

Perhaps the greatest inducement for change was the belief that release was earned through conformity and lost as a result of misconduct. Most of us had been committed to the PJR on an indefinite sentence. This meant that the day of departure was predicated on the administrator's perception of our readiness for return to society. If we "kept our nose clean" and displayed a mastery over former problems, our potential for freedom was increased.

There were other rewards, however. Token reinforcements served to validate achievements. Privileges were earned on the basis of merit. Those who displayed social and intellectual competence could, if they chose, attend downtown school. Weekend home visits were granted to students who made the honor roll. Downtown passes were available to those whose behavior warranted the opportunity. Letters were awarded for athletic participation. Plaques, medals, ribbons, and certificates signified successful involvement in extracurricular functions. There were many ways to gain recognition and experience a positive sense of self-realization within the total institutional milieu.

The cottage environment also promised the potential attainment of officially recognized status. Conduct and leadership were the primary qualities used to identify candidates for highly prized positions within the cottage. From shineline supervisor to head floorwalker, each rank in the officially recognized social order was a testament to how the adults perceived certain boys. High position, and the privileges that accompanied it, signified approaching release.

17

Of Time and Temperament

For eighteen months I was a resident at the Pennsylvania Junior Republic. During that year and a half many experiences influenced my behavior, giving rise to various forms and degrees of change. Some of the resulting modifications of perceptions and actions were socially consistent, others were not. Nonetheless, the experiences I had within that time span, which included most of my sixteenth and seventeenth years, helped me develop a stronger, more coherent self-concept. Confidence and competence grew as I gradually learned to master different aspects of my life.

Perhaps the first visible improvement was in my physical appearance. The acne infecting my face, neck, and upper body had long exerted a negative influence on me. I felt inferior because of my marred looks and was sensitive to the slightest stare, not to mention the remarks of the boys at the PJR who helped continue this negative self-image by calling me names like "crater face," "moon man," "zit face," and "pimple Jack." The administration helped alleviate the external symptoms by scheduling regular visits with a dermatologist. A regime of lotions, soaps, and antibiotics was prescribed and I was placed on a strict diet. I followed the doctor's advice to the letter. Within a few months my complexion was almost completely cleared. Scars remained, but very few pimples. The name-calling slowly came to a halt. Yet it was not merely the gradual disappearance of pimples that changed people's perception of me. Even though I was still a legitimate "crater face," I had filled out to a healthy six feet, 170 pounds. My size gave people a reason to view me differently. Boys were less prone to make nasty statements to someone who had grown more physically intimidating. A small amount of self-assuredness had crept into my life.

Academic success also came about at PJR. My performance in public school had long been borderline to failing. Due to lack of attendance, the first half of the tenth grade, which I had spent enrolled in the industrial course before commitment to the institution, had resulted in no grades. I was, therefore, a half year behind my classmates at the Republic. For the first time ever, I attempted to apply myself to an educational program. There were a number of reasons for this new approach: I no longer had to endure the home problems that sapped my concentration; my acne condition was improving, thus making me less self-conscious around other students; my new classmates had experienced educational difficulties similar to my own; my courses were less difficult; there was plenty of study time; the reward of weekends at home for making the honor roll was a strong incentive; good grades might also be a way to gain release; I wanted to pass the year and prove that I was not stupid.

I soon began to excel. Other students looked to me for answers and copied from my papers. Teachers complimented my work. The English teacher even went so far as to point out that I had some ability to express myself in writing. I devoured every positive remark, seeking to gain much desired recognition from what had formerly proved to be a failing. At the close of the school year my final grades were as follows: English II, B; World History, B; Biology, B; General Math II, B+. I was selected as the outstanding student of the tenth grade and given a certificate of merit. Mother came to the ceremony—her only visit to the institution. It was the first truly proud moment of my life.

During summer school I made up the half year of course work I had missed. My grades—English II, C+; World History, C; Biology, C; General Math II, B—were not as good as I would have liked but they were sufficient to fulfill all requirements for advancement to the eleventh grade.

Just before beginning junior year, I was asked if I wished to attend downtown school. After careful consideration, I declined. I still lacked confidence in both my intellectual abilities and my appearance. It seemed more prudent to remain where I had managed some success, rather than take a chance that could lead to failure.

My accomplishments at school encouraged the institutional administration to suggest I join the staff of the *Republic Citizen,* a monthly paper that related campus news. I quickly agreed for two specific reasons: positive comments from the English teacher had given me the incentive to go on with my writing and a staff position on the newspaper offered exposure to administrators who might find me worthy of release. I began as sports editor and later became feature editor. It was a wonderful experience and I took to it with increasing interest and dedication.

Junior year brought the best academic performance of my high school career. Spurred on by the recognition and pride earned during the tenth grade, I strived to do even better. Making good grades became a compulsion. I felt as though I had done poorly if my mark was not the highest in every test. At the end of the school year, my final grades were: English III, B+; American History, A−; World Geography, A; General Science III, A−; General Math III, A−. I was selected the outstanding student of the eleventh grade and labeled a "brain" by both teachers and peers. Confidence in my intellectual abilities was growing.

Certain leadership qualities also began to surface. Every Fourth of July the institution had a combination track, field, and swimming meet. Because I was the only boy within Prasse Hall experienced in competitive swimming, I was elected captain of the team. The meet was a nip and tuck struggle that found Main Hall, the perennial winner of all athletic events at PJR, vying with us for the championship. The point spread was so narrow that the winner would be decided by the last event, the freestyle relay. I was the anchor man. By the time the first three boys from Prasse had swum their legs, we were nearly one full length behind. I dove into the pool, stroked hard to the far end, did a flip turn, and swam back fast enough to beat the boy from Main Hall by a nose. We won the meet. The team cheered my effort.

Intramural sports thus provided me another means of distinguishing myself. I was chosen captain of the cottage basketball, volleyball, and softball teams. We won the championship in each. The coaches, who were also our teachers, asked me to try out for the campus teams. Especially insistent was the football coach, who believed the combination of mental and physical abilities made me a prime candidate for quarterback. I refused the offer. Though I had gained some belief in my athletic potential, I did not have the confidence to test my skills against the best athletes on campus, nor did I have the interest and dedication to attend daily practices. I did, however, agree to manage the baseball team.

My status on campus became more positive and more visible the more I learned to function and express myself within the confines of the institution. Inside the cottage I had become a leader. What proved to be a deciding factor in my own recogniton of the stature I had attained among my cottage mates became evident during an evening of civil defense drills. Twice a month each cottage marched around the lawn that faced the administration building practicing maneuvers designed to train us for action in case of a national emergency. Gino, the sadistic barber, was in charge of this event. We dreaded those evenings. Gino always found a reason to abuse at least one boy. One such evening, Gino commanded us to pretend the entire cottage was under attack. We were to pick a leader, march across the field, then figure a way back without him catching us. He was the enemy and would treat anybody and everybody he caught as prisoners. We knew what that meant. I was chosen leader.

In the darkness of the cool fall night, I devised a plan in which we were to split into two groups. One group would edge its way to the back of the administration building and work around to the far end. My group would bellycrawl to the opposite end of the field, then move between some buildings. That way Gino might only catch half of us. We would meet at the rear of the gymnasium and approach Gino from behind.

Gino stood like a great dark lump underneath the light at the entrance to the gymnasium as we dispersed. Thirty boys snaked forward on knees and elbows. Another thirty moved off in a different direction. Only the sound of cloth slithering across grass betrayed our presence as we crawled quietly through the shadows. An hour seemed to pass before we reached the buildings. I searched out Gino. He had not moved. We darted between the buildings and drew up behind the gymnasium. The other group soon joined us. Nobody had been spotted.

I told the others to wait, then crawled breathlessly toward Gino. A rock thrown toward the administration building diverted his attention. As he disappeared into the darkness to check the sound, I motioned the others to me. They approached quietly. Sixty beaming smiles greeted Gino's return. His response surprised us all. He was full of praise. I was given the credit. Even Gino had helped validate my newly emerging identity.

The cottage uncle offered further acknowledgement by advancing me through the officially recognized cottage hierarchy. I began as shineline supervisor, filled in as temporary floorwalker for a boy on vacation, became a full-time floorwalker several months later and, just before release, was promoted to head floorwalker. Each rung on the intercottage ladder of success brought increased responsibility and privileges, along with respect from peers and adults. In turn, my sense of self-worth grew more substantive. I was even selected cottage representative to the student government. Status had been attained through positive participation, achievement, and reinforcement within several areas of the officially recognized social order.

But not all aspects of my personality displayed signs of social conformity; nor had I managed to master certain aspects of my temperament. I was still suspicious of authority figures, manipulative, and physically aggressive. The basic survival mechanisms I had long clung to in an attempt to exercise some control over the environment had not yet developed into more mature responses.

There was one man I grew to dislike and mistrust—Reverend Bland, the institution's chaplain and supervisor of the detail on which I worked. We got along at first, but soon became adversaries. Perhaps some of my resentment toward him came from the many heated sermons I was subjected to by Nanan in her attempt to show me the error of my ways. I had never felt especially close to God, and moved even farther away each time the distance was pointed out. Reverend Bland did not enthrall me with his approach either. He always uncovered my shortcomings, never recognized my strengths. Every failure he saw in me became the subject of a personalized ministration that made me feel like the devil. I soon came to show him only my bad side. It seemed to be what he expected.

Twice I attempted to transfer to a different detail. At first I was put on the farm. Though I enjoyed the physical labor, there was no praise for my labors. On one hot late summer day spent baling hay I was one of three boys assigned the task of throwing the bales onto a truck. Two boys covered one side of the truck, I managed the other. I matched bale for bale with the two boys. When I asked the detail supervisor how I had done, seeking a compliment, he replied that I was "lazy" and could have done "more." I asked for another transfer within a week and was put in the carpentry shop. The dust irritated my skin. Pimples blossomed forth. I was reassigned to Reverend

Bland. We remained at odds until the day of my release. He never gave me the positive reinforcement I desperately needed and I declined to show him the respect he demanded.

But release was my primary concern. I did almost anything to achieve it. As people who have been institutionalized against their will know, departure is a constant thought. The ends justify the means. One learns to manipulate situations in order to influence control over results. I wrote letters to mother, Nanan, Mr. Lantz, and Judge Arkins highlighting my achievements while stressing my readiness for responsibility. During visits home I made certain to see Mr. Lantz or Judge Arkins in the hope that they would agree to release. Though most of these visits were spent on the streets, the last days always ended with me pleading for my freedom. It was my major goal in life. I wanted out at any cost.

I also learned to manipulate the institutional environment to gain advantages over certain situations. This was especially necessary in the areas of personal safety and identity. Aggression was the primary quality used to establish rank within the unofficial social order. Boys responded to each other according to relative unofficial ranking faster than officially recognized stature. It was a major consideration in choosing friends, in determining how to respond to other boys, and an important way to establish oneself. The most physically able boys had the best chance of not being exploited, harassed, or beaten by peers. The weak, and those who associated with them, were treated the harshest. It was an excellent example of the "survival of the fittest."

Fighting frightened me at first. There were so many aggressive boys who seemed to have no fear. Many appeared to enjoy it. I tried to avoid confrontations but that was impossible. There was always somebody who wanted to check me out. After a few fights I came to realize that the fear of being harmed, and the guilt feelings that ensued, were more damaging than the actual encounter. A few victories instilled confidence and gained respect from the other boys. Peer approval was something I truly desired. The years of being shunned and mocked by fellow students in public schools had left me starved for acceptance; it did not matter how I attained it. By the end of the first year I was considered the number one wheel in Prasse Hall. At release I perceived myself among the top ten on campus. I got to the point where I fought anybody at the drop of a hat. Toughness became a very important part of my identity.

It is difficult to remember how many fights I was involved in during that year and a half—a dozen, perhaps—but I will never forget the one that established me as a contender on campus. It happened at the intramural volleyball championship game that pitted Prasse Hall against our arch rival Main Hall. Prasse had won the last two championships and was about to sweep the third. It was a bitter prospect for the Main Hall players. For years they had won nearly every championship. Their cottage was considered the toughest on campus. The oldest and baddest guys were thrown together there. Their reputation was on the line.

After we had won the final point of the third and deciding game, a player from Main Hall came over and shoved me. I pushed him back. Suddenly my face was on fire as he hit me with a barrage of open-handed slaps. I swung back, though he got the best of me. A coach separated us before too much damage was done.

But the fight was not over. There was too much at stake. My honor and the honor of Prasse Hall had been challenged. Everybody in both cottages knew what had happened. To let the matter rest would be to admit that I lacked heart. I would lose my self-respect, my rep, my identity. Better to be beaten, than to give up.

That night brought little rest as I pondered what I had to do. I knew something about my adversary. His name was Bruno Packer. He was supposed to be a "War Lord" for a corner gang in Philly. He was my height, but fuller across the chest. He walked at the front of

Main Hall's line, which signified his status as a wheel. I had doubts as to whether I could beat him. Many of my cottagemates wagered against me.

The next day I passed the word that I wanted a "fair one." We would meet Saturday at noon in the men's room of the auto shop. Bruno quickly accepted.

With forced resolve, I stepped through the auto shop door in search of Bruno. Raised eyes and whispers registered my presence. Bruno looked up from beneath the hood of a '57 Ford wagon, his cool dark eyes glaring through me. He wrung a rag between his greasy fists. I underhanded a you-first gesture toward the men's room. Bruno flung the rag to the floor and ambled ahead of me.

The men's room door clicked closed behind us. Bruno turned to face me, his fists clenched into two black balls. I locked the door in defiance of his cocksureness. "Only one of us walks outa here," I announced full of my own false bravado. Bruno continued his unnerving silence. Our unblinking eyes were already deep in combat. Slowly, deliberately, I pulled off my gloves. Bruno appeared unimpressed. His hands were held high, his body turned in a boxer's stance.

Suddenly our fists were a whirlwind of knuckles in search of unprotected flesh. Pain raked my head, chest, and hands, my breath coming in burning gasps as Bruno and I wrestled and punched our way around the small room.

I lunged through the flurry and rammed him backwards until his head crashed into the cement block wall. As I caught him in a grinding headlock, he shoved me off balance, and we four-legged across the room. His head still imprisoned under my armpit, he slammed into the porcelain washstand that had been my target and crashed to the floor, blood gushing from a two-inch gash at his chin. The chrome spiggot rattled in the bowl.

"Had enough?" I gasped from above him.

Bruno spat. His trembling hands smeared blood across his face. He tried to stand.

A frantic thumping at the door stole my thunder. "Open this door! What's going on in there?"

The door's unlocking admitted a group of grease monkeys led by Uncle Blaze, the man in charge of the auto shop. They gaped at Bruno, then at me. I forced my way through the crowd and out into the cool, almost spring-like wind, rushing toward the cottage like a warrior returning home from battle, chin held high, all scrapes and bruises, swollen pride and swollen face, looking for recognition of my victory.

This was my level of development at the time of release. I had experienced quite a few changes, some more positive than others, and I had gained some strengths, succeeding in areas that had formerly been failures, uncovering abilities I did not know existed, and acquiring a certain amount of confidence and competence in controlling my life. The ensuing years would be the ultimate test of whether or not I would master my destiny or succumb to it.

18

Through Official Eyes

Institutional records register how other people viewed my psychological state and the ebb and flow of my progress during this period. Unfortunately, however, the commentaries are limited due to the fact that there were only three counselors on staff to accommodate over three hundred boys. Consequently, counseling was generally done in groups. Individual sessions were a rarity. The counselor/subject ratio made it nearly impossible to dig deeply into each boy's problems. Resultant commentaries provide predominantly gut-level responses to surface behavior that have been reduced to capsulized overviews.

On the other hand, Mr. Lantz continued in his role as probation officer and recorded his observations which reveal what was occurring within the home environment while I was at PJR and help explain some of the reasons why it was considered wise to have me remain at the institution for such a prolonged period of time.

EDUCATIONAL AND PSYCHOLOGICAL EXAMINATIONS
1–26–61

Essential High School Content Battery

Achievement Test	Percentile	Grade Level
English	67	10
Arithmetic	79	+10
Social Studies	42	10
Science	79	+10
Battery Median	73rd percentile	10th-grade equivalent

Summary of Behavior Check Lists

Mooney: Waln is able to recognize many of his basic problems but he lacks inner strength and insight to solve them. He feels entirely helpless. The chief concern is the home; he lacks respect for the grandparents and mother but has guilt to the point of persecution because of them. He verbalizes that he wants help but he lacks sufficient inner strength to seek it out. It will almost have to be thrust upon him.

Rorschach Summary: Waln is slightly retarded in his social, educational, and vocational development. There was nothing pathological in the picture except for a minimal tendency toward seeing rare details, and this is not at all out of proportion, although it gives him a slight odd-ball identification. He is extroverted and has good common sense, and is of high average intelligence. He has been an underachiever, and is capable of doing better work than his record indicates.

There was a slight weighting of space details with negativistic implications, and he is stubborn rather than hostile. He is sensitive and a little impulsive; but in general his control seems to be adequate.

I believe that Waln is an instance of unwarranted retardation due to family problems beyond his control and asynchronous growth patterns. A concern over his parents divorce and a desire to help his mother caused him to be inattentive to his own problems and growth needs. Certainly, he should finish high school and find a job consistent with his abilities. His problem is simply a maturity problem, and I feel that the Republic will supply an environment that will place emphasis on *his* development and *his* problems, and he should make a satisfactory adjustment.

Analysis of Figure Drawing: Waln is an "empty barrel" who has no inner strength or drive. He views the mother figure as overwhelming and domineering. He has built a shell around himself and crawled in—it would appear that this has been necessary in order to survive. He lacks insight. His personality is constricted and very flat. He is fearful and insecure. He lacks empathy for people.

Test Summary and Recommendation: Waln is a lad of normal intelligence, I.Q. 103, who is achieving scholastically at about expectancy. Waln is a very empty lad with no inner strength or drive. He holds himself in low esteem and lacks self-respect. He has strong feelings of guilt particularly about his resentment of his home situation. These guilt feelings have mounted to the point of self-persecution. He has many deepseated, neurotic tendencies. He needs a mature adult male with whom to identify. He is confused as to his sex role. He needs encouragement and strong motivation. Prognosis—fair.

COUNSELORS' REPORTS

2-28-61   Waln will come off orientation in a few days and be put into school. He has shed his tears since he has been here—yes—many of them, but he is actually beginning to stiffen up and to face life quite realistically. To be sure he does some salesman work but at least he is a good buyer. He is coming in good shape.

3-30-61   Waln is quite the kid. He needs an awful lot of personal attention. He feels his mother kept him tied too closely to her apron strings or else tried to and he will have none of it so therefore he rebelled but the strange thing is he wants attention. We have a thoroughly confused lad who needs a lot of pushing and a lot of encouragement because the inner strength is weak.

4-3-61   *Easter vacation report:* Waln came back on Sunday because Mrs. Trainer had to work today so she brought him today. Says he broke one rule— was out until 11:10 at a girl's house and forgot the time—a new girl friend he just met her that night. Reginald "Butchy" Frey, our ex-boy, was the oldest one there. They were coloring Easter eggs—3 girls and 6 boys. He met her at a little restaurant—she doesn't work there, just hangs around there. Says he got along wonderful with grandparents and mother. His mother told him that she thinks he is a man now. Attitude good. I hope all is what it appears to be on the surface.

4-28-61   Waln has been a sad sack this month, however, he can kid with you, and tells me I just imagine it so that part is good. He still is extremely immature with little inner strength. The acne is clearing but the shoulders and posture are still bad. We are not over the hump with him yet.

5-31-61   Waln is now out at work when he is not in school which is real good for him. I hear he can work, which is interesting. His attitude is good. His shoulders and posture are still bad so we are still not over the hump.

6-20-61   Went home June 9 to June 18. Got back at 8:00 P.M. Sunday. He says he didn't break any rules and spent most of the time with his family. They went bowling, swimming, to dinner, just sat around and talked. Says he saw some girls and had some informal dates. He got along wonderfully with his grandparents and the grandfather gave him $5. His attitude is good. His eyes are brighter than I have ever seen them.

6-30-61   Waln has come a long way, however, he is still immature but his attitude is good and he is pulling by the "boot straps" in good shape. The most he appears to need is time and guidance.

7-31-61   He contributes—still on the quiet side. Works best on an individual basis. Attitude good.

8-28-61   He has had a good month. He is still more quiet
than we like but his attitude is good and he is trying.

9-30-61   Waln has done a lot of fussing this month. He is
overly anxious for release. There are times when
he has been downright nasty. Mr. Gladden put him
back on Reverend Bland's detail because the other
place he was getting too much dust for his acne.
He still lacks respect for Reverend Bland and cannot seem to see most of the fault is within him. I
am not quite sure what the outcome of this lad will
be.

10-31-61   Waln has done a little better this month. He has finally accepted that he will be here until January.
Waln has been trying to manipulate everyone to
get another boy moved up to Prasse but to no
avail. He is really a persistent lad when he gets
started on anything regardless of what it is or the
outcome.

11-28-61   Waln has had some month again. Mr. Gladden has
him on Reverend Bland's detail and they surely are
not getting along. Reverend Bland came up com-
plaining he was insolent, leans on the furniture and
sleeps and would do no work, etc. Waln says it is
not true and I do not know. He surely has no respect for Reverend Bland. I am trying to tell him to
get along with all kinds of people and cooperate
but he says this one is impossible.

12-20-61   Waln was assigned to my group a week ago. I've seen him once and must get to know him better before giving a fair report. He appears to lack drive, ambition, and long term goals.

1-2-62   Waln was home 12–22 to 1–2. His mother has been in the hospital and is going back January 8—heart operation. She is getting along OK. New Years Eve he was across the street at his buddy's house until 12:30. He says the grandparents want him back. He saw his P.O. who said he was glad with the way Waln is doing but didn't say anything about release. He came back willingly. Waln's attitude is good.

1-24-62   Waln is still sizing up the situation. In counseling he says little but is attentive. I took Waln and four others to a basketball game in Mercer and he acted like a perfect gentleman. My main complaint is that Waln lacks inner strength and drive. On the surface his attitude is good.

2-28-62   Waln appears to be coming nicely in all respects. He is now responding to all that is good and appears to be sincere. He lacks self-esteem but is nevertheless a pleasure. His attitude is good.

3-21-62   Waln continues to be cooperating in all respects. I hope it isn't just a surface effect. The only complaint at the present is Waln's lack of drive and enthusiasm. His attitude is good.

4-23-62   Left about 10:00 A.M. on 4–19. Boy from Middletown came for him. Came back 4–23 with the

same boy. Broke one rule and said he was out until
11:30. Friday night he was at a girl's house. Said he
mostly stayed at home during his vacation. Got some
candy, a suit, and shoes, etc. Said he didn't go to
church because his mother was sick. Had Easter
dinner with his family. Attitude seemed fairly good.

4-30-62   Mr. Gladden gave me Waln back this month. I was
quite shocked when I found his eyes were dull
and heavy as ever. He was as a withered flower again.
The only thing he complains about is Reverend
Bland's detail. Otherwise he is just putting in time.

5-31-62   Waln still not back to where he was. He is still
listless and still concerned about going home.
He creates no problems but neither does he do anything worthwhile. I am worried about this guy.

YORK COUNTY JUVENILE PROBATION OFFICE
PROBATION RECORD

January 1961   **Placement at Republic:** On the 13th arrangements
were made for Waln's transfer from the Detention
Receiving Facility to the Pennsylvania Junior Republic Association.

March 1961   **Hearing Regarding Support:** Mr. Brown appeared
before the Hon. George W. Arkins in Juvenile Court
on Thursday afternoon, March 23. We had not advised Mrs. Brown to be present and Judge Arkins
indicated that he thought it would be best if both

parents would be present, as any modifications of the present support order ought to be made in the presence of both individuals. He accordingly set Thursday, March 30, at 2:00 P.M., as the time for Mr. and Mrs. Brown to appear before him.

Follow-up Hearing: Mr. and Mrs. Brown appeared before Judge Arkins on the afternoon of March 30. Mr. Brown testified that he was paying $35 a week to Mr. Garner's office for the support of his wife and three children. Later Mr. Garner confirmed this report. He told the judge he was a cab driver and that on the side he operates Employment Associates, an employment agency with offices on East Market Street. He produced his recent income tax so that the judge might understand what his earnings are. He stated that he lives with his parents.

Judge Arkins spoke very briefly with Mrs. Brown and learned from her that she is gainfully employed.

Judge Arkins then directed that there would be no change in the amount of the order, but he directed a different distribution. In short, $5 per week is to be turned over to the county as partial reimbursement for Waln's maintenance at the Republic. When he returns to the community the Juvenile Probation Department is to notify the adult division, at which time an appropriate order will be made by the judge.

Following the hearing Waln had an Easter visit with Judge Arkins. He told the judge he was in the tenth grade in the academic program and that he liked it.

Judge Arkins complimented him on how much his acne condition had cleared. The boy told the judge that this summer they were going to do some superficial sanding to remove the scars.

April 1961   *Visit at Boy's Home:* We called at the home on the afternoon of the 25th and spoke with Waln's grandparents. We learned that his mother had resigned from her employment with Dr. Pleasant and at the time of our visit was resting. It seems that she has been ill and has been doctoring with several M.D.s. Dr. Samuels' name was mentioned by Mr. and Mrs. Strine. During the visit they told us that her nerves were in pretty bad shape. We made arrangements with them to have Mrs. Brown call us in the event an emergency develops.

June 1961   On the 1st we received a report from Mr. Gladden that Waln is entitled to a summer vacation between June 9 and September 1. We immediately wrote, giving our permission for such a visit. The family is to make their own arrangements.

We learned that Waln's mother recently visited the Republic and that she was delighted with the school and that Waln had been placed on the honor roll. She hopes that he can be kept at the school until he can develop a new set of values.

Visit from Boy: On the 16th Waln came to the office early in the morning. He advised us that he had been given a vacation, that he had arrived in York on the evening of the 9th. He said that he arrived at the Harrisburg Interchange with a boy who had been released from the institution and was en route to Philadelphia. Waln is to be back at the institution on Sunday evening, the 18th, at 8:00 P.M. so that he can enroll in a summer school course on Monday morning, the 19th.

During this visit, Waln told us that his mother was again working for Dr. Pleasant. He said he thought she had gone back about a month ago. We complimented Waln on how well he looked and especially about the way he had handled his acne condition as it had practically cleared up. During this visit he told us that he had recently been put on the school paper and that he would keep us informed of other achievements. Following our visit, he spent a few minutes talking with Judge Arkins.

September 1961

Visit at School: We visited with Waln and the faculty at the Republic on the 14th. Waln told us he had recently returned from a nine day visit at home. He said he had had a few dates, had gone to the movies, played softball, and did some swimming. He readily admitted he was not at home as much as he should have been. He said his mother financed the trip. While visiting with Waln, he said he had been at the Republic nearly eight months, that he is in the eleventh grade and is now ready to come home, register in senior high and graduate. In the same breath he said he wanted to lighten the load for his mother. When we questioned him concerning this he told us he meant to get a job so she would not have to carry so much of the responsibility for the home. At this point we told Waln that the best thing he could do to lighten his mother's burden was to develop some firm convictions about the way he was going to behave and then stick to them.

He also asked us if he could go home with one of the other boys during the weekend of September 15–16–17 so that he could attend the York Fair. In addition, he told us he wanted to talk with Judge Arkins about letting him stay home and register in public school. It was our impression that this young man is definitely a chip off the old block and emulates his parents, who are definitely schemers. We told Waln that the matter of having him come home was entirely up to the authorities at the school.

Telephone Call from Mother: We spoke with Mrs. Brown on the 22nd, advising her of our visit with her son and that in our opinion he is still manipulating the authorities at the school and had tried it with us. She readily agreed that Waln was not ready to come home. She pointed out that when he was home for a visit he spent little time there until the last day of the stay, then he became interested in having her do something about having him released. She admitted she was almost helpless.

November 1961   On the morning of the 15th Mrs. Brown came to the office. She looked ghastly white and spoke in almost inaudible monotones. She said she had been hospitalized during October, that they found some precancerous lesions in her mouth and an aggravated cardiac condition. She told us that she borrowed money from Waln's twelve-year-old brother Lee's savings from his paper route to pay for Waln's plane fare from the Republic to York and return. He is scheduled to arrive in York on the evening of the 17th and return to the Republic on the 19th.

Mrs. Brown continues to work for Dr. Pleasant. We got the impression from Mrs. Brown that neither she or her parents are up to managing Waln at this time; neither could take any additional worries. Both families appear to be going downhill fast.

It would seem to us that it would be to Waln's advantage to accept as much training as the Republic can make available to him and better prepare himself to face the realities of life.

Mrs. Brown wrote us on the 18th that she arrived at Temple University Hospital on Friday, November 25, that she underwent a number of blood tests and numerous X-rays. We immediately acknowledged her letter and tried to assure her that she was in good hands and that we would take care of her son, Waln.

December 1961

Christmas Vacation Arrangements: Mrs. Strine, Waln's grandmother, called early in the morning of the 15th. She said she would like to give Waln a Christmas present of a trip home. She also advised that Waln's mother was going to be brought home from the hospital on the 16th or 17th by Dr. Pleasant. She will have to return to the hospital at a later date for further surgery.

Waln visited us on the afternoon of the 19th. He
had a terrible cold. He told us that the Republic
thought for a time that he would not be able to
make it home for Christmas. He recalled that he
came home by car with Gary Reidel of Mechanics-
burg on December 22nd and that he is expected
back at the Republic on January 2 at 4:00 P.M.

Waln told us that it was good to get home to see
his mother and grandparents. He has spent his
Christmas vacation going to the movies and "loafing" at a girlfriend's house.

He reported that he is on Reverend Bland's detail at
the Republic and that he likes it. At the moment,
he is registered in the eleventh grade and has been
getting good grades. His acne condition has cleared
up considerably. He still has two large eruptions on
the back of his neck. The youngster is now approximately 6' tall and weighs in the neighborhood of
170 lbs.

During this visit, Waln indicated to us that he has
been thinking very seriously of completing his high
school work, going on to college and becoming a
social worker.

He seemed very concerned over the fact that his
mother owes $1,000 to the York department stores
and that recently she had a bill for $485.00 from
the Income Tax Department. We told Waln to advise his mother that we would see what we could
do to intervene for her with the Tax Department
but could do nothing about her personal obligations to the department stores.

Mother Visits Office: Mrs. Brown came to the office and reported that her son had sent her in because "we" supposedly wanted to talk with her. We told Mrs. Brown that we would never have done such a thing because we knew of her weakened condition. We tried to figure out with Mrs. Brown's help why Waln had done this.

She is still thin, speaks in an almost inaudible undertone, and walks as though she might have suffered a mild stroke. She told us that she is to return to the hospital early in January, is to be seen in the heart clinic at Temple Hospital, and there is a possibility that they might resort to heart surgery. When we spoke with her about her unsteady gait, she readily admitted that the physicians at the hospital had indicated that she might have suffered a stroke, and she went on to relate that the right part of her side might be slightly paralyzed.

January 1962

On January 16th, Waln wrote separate letters— one to us and one to Judge Arkins, telling us that he would like to come home to accept his family responsibilities as he now feels that he is the head of the family. We acknowledged our correspondence and also the letter addressed to Judge Arkins.

June 1962

Furlough: Waln came to the office on the afternoon of the 11th. He reported that he arrived in York on the 9th. He said that Luther Davis's parents brought him home from the Republic on a furlough. Dr.

Pleasant is planning to get him employment. During the visit, he advised us that he had received straight A's except for a B plus in History. He has completed the 11th grade. In September he is planning on enrolling at the York Suburban High School in a college preparatory course.

19

A Period of Adjustment

Upon release from the PJR, I was returned to the custody of the family and the watchful eye of the County Probation Office. The transition was not easy. Twenty-one of the previous twenty-four months of my life had been spent in institutions. I had had only fleeting contacts with the outside world. There was still much confusion raging in me and, of course, the difficulties at home had not vanished. Though Mother was back to work at the dentist's office, she was visibly unwell. The leukemia was steadily killing grandad. Nanan was "sick with worry" over them both, clinging ever more desperately to "God's word" as her final way of coping. It was a critical period, a point in time when I could easily have gotten into more trouble and been reinstitutionalized.

Fortunately, however, there were several positive influences that helped to insulate me during this vulnerable period. Perhaps the most prominent among them was the acquisition of a certain amount of maturity. The eighteen-month confinement at the PJR had occurred during a critical period in my development. I had learned some valuable lessons, and had adjusted my behavior accordingly. Thus, I was psychologically better equipped to handle the environment that had helped to cause my original downfall.

There was also a deep desire not to be locked away again. Freedom is a terrible thing to lose. My eighteenth birthday was nearing and after that I would be "tried" as an adult.

The family situation had become slightly more manageable. Though sickness and old age still infected the household, the initial shock of trying to deal with so many problems had passed. The family had gained some stability. Lee and Carolyn were older, more self-sufficient. As a result of these changes, there was a somewhat less confused home environment to rekindle my need to rebel.

Another major influence during this period came through meeting a new group of friends. I knew that if I began to loaf with the old gang again it would mean trouble. Trouble was something I didn't want. After all, I was still on probation and had learned that Mr. Lantz knew my every movement. He checked on my progress—regularly.

It was two of the neighborhood kids, though, who were most instrumental in helping me to meet new friends. Jim, who lived in the other side of our semi-detached house, was sixteen. Jerry, who was fifteen, lived five houses away. The three of us, plus the other four brothers in our families, had been playmates through our early years but had drifted apart during the period when family problems had caused me to seek the company of boys who more closely mirrored my inner feelings. Jim and Jerry introduced me to their friends. Even though I looked quite different from them, with my greased hair and other "hood" trappings, most of my new acquaintances came to accept me. Soon I had begun to look more "Ivy League" and was starting to develop a different attitude toward life.

Six weeks after returning home, I took a dishwashing job at a local restaurant. The hours were four until midnight, six days a week. It was my first real job. Although the take-home pay was only thirty-six dollars a week, I was able to give mother money and still have enough left to buy clothes and save for a car. I was finally able to contribute to the maintenance of the family and establish a small sense of financial independence. Another important thing about the job was that it kept me off the streets at night. I had a place to be and a reason to be there.

Only once that summer did I almost get into trouble. One evening when several of my new friends and I were driving around looking for something to do, a carload of beer-guzzling trouble-makers pulled beside us and asked if we were "looking for a fight." We said "no," but that made no difference. They kept shouting and throwing beer bottles at us until the driver of our car—Andy, a football player known for his short fuse—got tired of being harassed and challenged them to a fight. In dead silence we drove to the parking lot of a restaurant to do battle. I did not want to get into a fight and maybe get in trouble with the police, but I could not abandon my new friends at such a moment. There was no choice. All of a sudden the beer-guzzlers were swinging and I was in the middle of it. Within a few minutes the fight was over, the police were summoned, and an ambulance was brought for two of the beer-guzzlers. Aware that I was on probation, my new friends shielded me from the questions of the police. Yet tales about the fight soon spread. Summer ended shortly thereafter.

Returning to public school was the next difficult adjustment. It was my senior year and I had been returned to the school district that had first expelled me. Other circumstances further complicated the situation. The school district was considered the wealthiest in the county. Jaguars, Corvettes, Cadillacs, and other expensive cars lined the school parking lot, offering a graphic contrast to the '49 Chevy I had bought with dishwashing money. To make matters worse, my reputation as a reform school graduate and fighter had become common knowledge. Within weeks I had begun living up to the reputation and by Christmas I was considered the toughest kid in the high school. Fighting was still a very important part of my identity. It was the one thing I knew I could do well, my way of gaining respect and acceptance.

The educational program at school also became a problem.

The school district took pride in academic excellence, sending a large percentage of its graduates on to college. I had become accustomed to the less demanding program at the PJR and, therefore, was not prepared for such subjects as psychology, chemistry, Spanish, Health and senior English. By the second marking period I had dropped Chemistry and Health, replacing them with wood shop and study hall. I failed Spanish. Despite these pitfalls, I graduated, ranking 187th in a class of 192. I had to remain in school a week after the other seniors had departed in order to make up quite a few hours of detention and if it had not been for a remarkable adeptness at cheating, I would have failed psychology and senior English and, ultimately, flunked the year. Nonetheless, graduation marked the first plateau in my life. I was proud of the accomplishment.

Yet graduation was not achieved merely through desire. There were other influences. Mr. Detweiler, the high school principal who had been involved during my original school difficulties, had taken a personal interest in my education. Though he had had a thousand opportunities to expel me or otherwise make my school experience miserable, he had provided me every possible chance to complete the year. The English teacher had also taken time to offer his support and interest. With their subtle guidance and the supervision of the County Probation Office, I managed to acquire an unearned sheepskin.

Graduation presented the ultimate goal for which I had striven: FREEDOM. No more hours wasted in classes. No more imposed schedules. No more teachers to give detention. I was even, finally, off probation. Except for mother, there was nobody to tell me what to do. I was a man, free to make my own choices. But I knew little about options, or how to use them wisely. I did not know how to plan for the future, most of my life having been structured for me. I was soon in a tailspin.

Two weeks after graduation I found a job as a laborer in a textile mill and lost it within four weeks when I suffered a 220-volt electrical shock at the mill and was unable to return for work the remainder of the week. Unable to produce employment in the ensuing weeks and with no idea what else to do, I tried to join the Army, thinking they would teach me a trade and maybe send me to Officer's Candidate School. The recruiter said that I "could build a future in the military." But an Army future was not to be. I was quickly classified 1-Y, then 4-F, and denied military induction for "psychological reasons." The past had caught up with me. Rejection from military service was a severe blow. Even Uncle Sam did not "want" me. The old feelings of failure and rejection were coming back again.

For the next two years I moved aimlessly through industry, losing job after job. No work captured my interest. I was constantly falling asleep, holding up the assembly line, running the machines incorrectly, late for work, absent from work, or committing some other unacceptable offense. No less than ten employers saw fit to fire me within those two years.

At first mother was understanding. She knew that it would take time to find my "niche." But even a mother's patience does not last forever, especially when money is needed. Grandad had died during my senior year and Nanan within a year after my graduation, which brought an end to the Social Security pension checks that had helped to maintain us all. The support payment from father had been reduced after the arrival of my eighteenth birthday. The only remaining sources of income were the support payment for Lee and Carolyn and mother's small income as a dental assistant. This made the repeated absence of my contribution an added strain on the already inadequate family budget. The "worry over money" had finally impressed me with its full meaning. I was the "man of the house" and still unable to handle the responsibility.

I sought escape through a nightly blur of barrooms and fistfights, undirected and unable to resolve the feelings of inadequacy that had plagued me since childhood. Everything I did seemed to turn to failure. There was nothing to hold on to. Age twenty-one was drawing ever closer. I was supposed to be a "man," capable of making my way in the world. What was I going to do with my life?

The month before my twenty-first birthday I enrolled in York Junior College. Nothing else had worked. Maybe an education held the answer. In four years I could become a teacher—or something. Then I would have a profession. Mother readily bought the idea since she had always wanted me to further my education. She would somehow manage without my contribution as long as I studied hard and paid my bills.

I applied for an educational loan and, due to family income, was also granted participation in a work-study program supervised by the dean of students, who offered flexible hours and provided support and direction so that I would profit from a college experience. But I was still not up to the task. Poor study habits and the party atmosphere of college life soon took their toll. By the end of the first semester I had earned a shaky 1.6 cumulative average. As a result, I became ineligible for the work-study program and was placed on academic probation.

The second semester was no better than the first. Once again the dean offered his encouragement, finding me a part-time job in industry. By the end of the second semester I had developed a severe case of pyorrhea, lost the part-time job, and dropped to a 1.4 semester average, which brought my cumulative average down to a 1.5. I was continued on academic probation. At least I had completed the year without being formally dismissed, however. I resolved to return the next term and do better.

The end of freshman year brought with it the need for summer employment. Within a week I found a job at a furniture store as a helper on the delivery truck. It was the perfect summer job: the people were nice, the pay was satisfactory, there was variety in the daily schedule, and the work was enjoyable. I did so well, or so I thought, that by the end of the first month the store owner asked me to become a salesman. He said that I had ability and could have a good future in the furniture business. I immediately accepted his offer. I thought that I had found my "niche."

A few weeks following the promotion I met Sally. There had been a handful of girls in the past, fleeting encounters that only reflected my sense of being unworthy, but nothing even slightly serious. For the first time I cared enough to fight the lack of self-confidence and the fear that had long forbidden even the thought of love and the potential for rejection that accompanied it. We spent every possible moment together, mingling our thoughts and dreams. I was alive with happiness. Somebody loved me.

Fall came much too quickly. While Sally went to Philadelphia to study interior design, I remained at the furniture store, giving up all thought of college for a more immediate dream. We had decided to be married after Sally's graduation and to work together in the furniture business. The future finally seemed to be beginning to take shape—until it became apparent that the furniture store owner with his pawing hands and promises of gifts for "favors," was not concerned with my salesmanship. By my twenty-second birthday I was once again in search of a career.

Three months later I was also without Sally. City life, and the stimulation of nearby university students, had changed her outlook with regard to her "future" with me. At our final meeting, she informed me that I was "dull," that I was "uneducated," that I never "read anything," and that she had found another boyfriend.

The devastation lasted for months. Job loss could be dealt with, but losing Sally's love was too much. The storybook future had been replaced by the bitter past. I lost weight, gnawed by self-pity and thoughts of suicide. If it had not been for the timely occurrence of three specific events, it is hard to guess what might have happened. My life was about to change for the better.

The first and most important of these events was mother's re-marriage, which lifted the responsibility as "man of the house" from my shoulders. I immediately moved to an apartment—lonely, but with a new sense of freedom.

The second event came at almost the same time. The sales experience at the furniture store made it possible for me to find employment with the local Sears as a vacuum cleaner and sewing machine salesman. With the job, my anguish over Sally had to give way to the reality of customer relations.

The third event involved my best friend, a college student whose intelligence I respected. He appeared to understand everything, while it seemed I could grasp nothing. One day he looked me squarely in the eyes and asked if I was going to be a "dumb fuck" the rest of my life, or whether I was going to start using my head. He then handed me Voltaire's *Candide* and told me to read it. Because of my respect for him, and my desire to prove that I was neither "dumb" nor "dull," I labored through the pages, unable to grasp the symbolism yet fascinated by the story line. The book seemed to be telling me something. Was this really the "best of all possible worlds?" Was there a better side to life? I began to seek answers to these questions. Books became my source of reference. A thirst for knowledge soon replaced the feelings of loneliness and rejection. Liberation from family duty and lost love had begun. I resolved to learn and experience more.

The summer before my twenty-third birthday, five years following release from reform school, my life began to gather direction. Taking the advice of Horace Greeley, I moved west to Los Angeles, California. It was a brand new world, a fresh beginning, a final separation from the past. I was free to fail or succeed according to my own abilities. There were no external pressures or responsibilities to weigh me down. Within two weeks I found a job in sales. By the fall I had enrolled for part-time classes in a junior college. New friends, new experiences, and minor successes in sales and college made that year a critical period of transition in my life. I had met life on even terms, and won.

The year of self-discovery in California came to an end when a letter from Sally declared that she "loved" and "missed" me. I rushed home to claim her thinking we would be married and live "happily ever after." But hope was, once again, put to rest. A blissful night together was followed the next day by a telephone call wherein Sally informed me that she was engaged to be married, that she was sorry, but that she had just had to see me one last time. It was an unexpected shock, but not devastating. Life had to go on. There was a new dream to be fulfilled. The desire for a college education had become all-consuming.

Shortly after my return to the East I found a job as a driver for an airfreight service. That fall I re-entered York Junior College and continued working full-time for the airfreight service. I studied and worked harder than ever before in my life. By the end of the academic year I had acquired sixty credits, raising my cumulative average to 2.13. I was graduated that spring with an Associate of Science degree in the liberal arts.

The sense of accomplishment I felt after completing the two-year degree gave me the incentive to continue the educational experience. At age twenty-four I had finally proven to myself that if I worked hard at something I could succeed. That fall I matriculated to junior status at the nearby Capitol Campus of the Pennsylvania State University, where I pursued a degree in the humanities. Classical literature and philosophy had captured my interest. Every spare moment was spent absorbing the writings of the masters in these disciplines. I reduced my hours at the airfreight service and took course overloads each term, including summer. Within a year and a half I received a baccalaureate degree—with highest distinction.

The following summer I began graduate courses at the University of Pennsylvania. My interest in classical literature and philosophy had broadened to include folklore and anthropology, especially the role of man in culture. By spring of the next year I was granted the degree of Master of Arts. The following year I had completed all requirements, except the dissertation, for the Ph.D.

At this point in my life, eleven years after release from reform school, I once again came in contact with juvenile justice and delinquency. Professor Kenneth Goldstein, who knew a little about my past, suggested that an anthropological approach to the study of juvenile delinquency could prove to be an excellent dissertation topic. I had never considered investigating this aspect of man in culture, delinquency being a part of the past I preferred to forget. Since Professor Goldstein was chairman of my graduate group as well as chairman of my dissertation committee, however I considered his suggestion a commandment.

After a summer with the airfreight service I found a position at the Pennsylvania Department of Education, which was then in the process of assuming full responsibility for providing educational services to delinquent children in Commonwealth-operated institutions. For the next three years I helped administer, coordinate, and design correctional education programs for delinquents. At the same time, I researched and wrote my dissertation *Gangways: An Expressive Culture Approach to Understanding Gang Delinquency*. My thesis was to explain how participation in Philadelphia's gang subculture provided a means for young blacks to gain recognition and support, attain success, and learn the intricacies of the lifestyle of inner-city ghetto existence. In the spring of 1976 I was awarded the Ph.D. degree.

The opportunity to study the literature pertaining to delinquency and to work with a variety of juvenile justice professionals during that three-year period was quite a learning experience. What struck me most was the atmosphere of negativism, defeatism, impotence, and gloom pervading both the theoretical and applied aspects of juvenile justice and delinquency. Growing numbers of young people were being shuffled through juvenile courts and institutions. Child care professionals were dismayed by their inability to provide the services necessary to inspire a socially acceptable behavioral change in their clients. The research literature framed its findings in recidivism rates and emphasized continued pathology. The media accentuated juvenile "injustice" and condemned all those responsible for "rehabilitation" as fostering "debilitation." Nowhere was a glimmer of hope to be found. It seemed that once a child was adjudged a delinquent and placed in the custody of the juvenile justice system, he or she was condemned to a life of problems that could only lead to further interventions and institutionalizations. Yet how could that be? I had been enmeshed in the juvenile justice system for most of my adolescence and somehow had come to enjoy a relatively normal adulthood. Was I, in some way, different? I began to reflect on my past.

But what had happened during childhood was no longer fresh in my mind. In order to jog my memory I began to collect and analyze all the extant documentation that chronicled my youth, particularly that of intervening agencies and institutions. Nearly one hundred fifty pages of official records were retrieved. Review of the documents brought forth long-repressed memories of a way of life that seemed alien, insurmountable. Recorded comments painted a bleak picture of my early life and anticipated future. Crushed and embittered by the negative appraisals of my potential, I set out to uncover the positive aspects of my development. The one essential question that had to be answered was how I had managed to survive and overcome so disturbed a childhood. I began to retrace my life from beginning to present. Mother died just prior to my starting the investigation.

Six months after beginning my personal project I was offered a position at the National Center for Juvenile Justice, whose director, E. Hunter Hurst, was interested in undertaking a research project entitled "Positive Outcomes"—an attempt to understand how and why some former juvenile offenders had managed to overcome their delinquent careers. The project fit perfectly with my personal research.

For nearly a year I searched the literature for clues into the process of delinquency abandonment. Only a handful of antecdotal, superficial, or, often, conflicting reports were to be found. I was shocked. There were voluminous references and theories describing the reasons for acquiring and maintaining a delinquent career, but next to nothing regarding its abandonment.

The following year I located nine former juvenile offenders and asked them to share their personal experiences with respect to becoming delinquent and overcoming delinquency. Through their personal, often painful, disclosures, it became apparent that there was much to be gained from this area of inquiry. It was at the completion of the "Positive Outcomes" project that I decided to invest my full energy into writing this book. Perhaps such a personal disclosure would tempt people to look at the other, more positive, side of delinquency.

20

The Other Side
of Delinquency

The factors that resulted in my delinquent adaptation are not especially unique. Each year thousands of young people suffer similar experiences. A disrupted or otherwise unstable home environment is often at the root of the problem. Some of these children develop a delinquent response that is considered sufficiently apparent to require intervention. Others manage to be less affected by their predicament. Some go undetected. Of those who become officially recognized as delinquent, some maintain their deviant patterns of behavior into adulthood, while others abandon their delinquent life-style and develop a more socially-consistent way of life. The literature is full of explanations regarding the development and maintenance of delinquency but offers, as I have said, practically nothing that sheds light on its abandonment.

It is my belief that delinquency is a dynamic form of behavior that is neither irreversible or unresolvable. Just as there are specific, identifiable causes for the evolution of a delinquent response, there are traceable reasons for its devolution. It is my further belief that by gaining an understanding of how and why some former juvenile offenders have managed to overcome their delinquent careers, it will be possible to develop intervention strategies, therapeutic programs, and other supportive mechanisms designed to help promote change. This chapter is an attempt to highlight the reasons for my own behavioral transformation.

But first a word of caution. This retrospective analysis is a subjective recounting of one man's life. It should not be considered a universal statement. I do not presume to know what is representative nor what is unique. Only with the accumulation and analysis of information gained from other individuals who have experienced a similar change of behavior will it be possible to identify patterns offering insights into the reasons for delinquency abandonment. From such insights we may be able to help current and future delinquents overcome their difficulties.

Early identification of my reaction to family problems was the preliminary step leading toward eventual resolution. The first grade teacher who considered me "moody" was the initial person outside the family unit to officially acknowledge that something was amiss. Upon her advice, I was taken to a child psychologist.

Early diagnosis resulted from the findings of the child psychologist, who identified the causes of my problems and made the family and others aware of the reasons for my behavioral reactions. Though he was not able to effect a change in my behavior, nor significantly alter the family situation, he did offer a point of reference that helped others understand what motivated my abnormal behavior. This information, in turn, provided insights regarding how to approach my problems.

Official intervention was necessitated by my increased deviance. The involvement of the juvenile court was the first dramatic commitment to a correction of the situation. It was well-timed. Though I rebelled against the intrusion of this agency, it is now apparent that without such help my problems would have continued unchecked. The ultimate outcome could have been far more devastating and difficult to correct if nothing had been opposed to the momentum of my deepening psychological and behavioral crisis. The juvenile court, through the efforts of the Juvenile Probation

Office, was able to exercise an element of control and provide an objective analysis of the situation. Neither of these mechanisms existed within a household crushed by difficulties. The Juvenile Probation Office could not solve problems, but it could monitor them, and when my rebellion became too radical, it was part of a larger system of services designed to diagnose and correct the disorder. Though I do not agree with all of the techniques used by this system pertaining to my case, it was, nonetheless, this system that initiated the "recovery" process.

Removal from the source of difficulties proved to be the ultimate approach to my predicament. The home environment had only served to stimulate my negative behavior. If an appropriate alternative placement had not been found, I suspect that both the family and I would have suffered much greater difficulties. My life might have gone unrepaired. Yet there were two mistakes that occurred during this process. The first had to do with the Lutheran Home. Mother's decision to put me there was wise and, had she stuck with it, probably would have had a positive long-range effect since I might not have been exposed to some of the experiences that ensued. Unfortunately, her inability to follow through only confused the matter and helped bring about the feelings of rejection I suffered as I was moved from one alternative setting to another. The second mistake was my commitment to the state hospital, also a devastating experience. It was apparent that I needed psychiatric help, but that never really happened. The diagnoses of the clinical staff only labeled the obvious without offering more than a superficial insight. Instead of helping to resolve my psychological conflicts, this placement, which left me immersed in filth and sickness, only served to compound my delusions. No human being, least of all a child, should be subjected to such an environment. I left the state hospital completely disillusioned and wondering if I was insane.

A more appropriate placement was found at the Pennsylvania Junior Republic. Though there are a number of less than positive aspects of mass-congregate institutionalization, the long-range effect proved beneficial in my case. For the first time in many years my life had structure. A well-defined, though harsh, disciplinary code put restrictions on my behavior. I was expected to attend school, taught to handle responsibility and provided opportunities to experience successes commensurate with the application of newly discovered abilities. I learned that I was capable of exercising control over the environment. In short, I was given a chance to mature. Had the court not interceded and secured appropriate placement during this crisis period, the potential for recovery would have been diminished.

Length of stay at the PJR was critical for three particular reasons. First, because my prolonged absence offered some relief to the adults at home who did not have to expend their energy dealing with my behavior and so found more time to deal with their own problems. Second, because of the continuous exposure to one environment and its treatment philosophy, I was given the necessary time to internalize an alternative approach to life. A shorter placement, rather than having any positive long-range effect, might only have created further confusion and instability. Third, I was able to achieve an educational plateau whereby, on release, I had only one year left in order to graduate. Had the amount of time been longer before I could reach this exceptionally important goal, there would have been an increased risk of my not attaining it.

Return to a more stable home environment was of great importance. What had been accomplished at the PJR could have been erased by re-entry into the same environment that had given rise to my rebellion. Though the atmosphere was not by any stretch of the imagination stable, it was less overtly pathological and, as a result, less prone to force me to renew my former defense mechanisms.

Some problems still remained, and I reacted to them in ways that reflected my concern, but because they were relatively less profound my reaction to them was proportionately less severe. Without such an alteration in the home environment, the potential to accomplish a behavioral change might have been severely diminished, if not destroyed.

Peer group change. Throughout my stay at the PJR I was advised that should I revert to my "old ways" after release, I would probably be reinstitutionalized. It was further impressed on me that the type of friend I chose would have an important bearing in determining the direction of my future. Though I realized the truth of these statements, had it not been for my opportune access to a new group of friends, and my acceptance by them, I would probably have renewed former acquaintances and former patterns of behavior. As a result of the establishment of new relationships with individuals whose approach to life was more socially conforming, I was able to select, emulate, and synthesize patterns of conduct I perceived more appropriate to increased social acceptance.

The supervision and support of many people proved imperative after release, especially during the first year following institutionalization. Most noteworthy among these people were Mr. Lantz, Mr. Detweiler and my mother. Mr. Lantz held a tight rein on my activities, monitoring my progress in school while at the same time offering guidance and praise where necessary. He became the strong authority figure I had needed throughout my adolescence. Mr. Detweiler provided a similar role in that he not only supervised my school behavior but also gave me many "second chances" in order that I might graduate. Mother's role was less direct, more enduring because she never quit believing I was capable of "better things." Other people, as well, never faltered in their support. The continued belief and interest of so many concerned people stimulated incentive to strive for higher goals.

Graduation from high school was one of my first major long-term accomplishments. Though I did not earn the diploma through conscientious study and dedication, I did have the desire and the opportunity to reach this goal. Had I been expelled, or otherwise thwarted in this endeavor, my chances to overcome immediate and future obstacles would have been gravely restricted. Furthermore, this one major accomplishment became the cornerstone upon which I was eventually able to construct a positive self-image.

Changing place of residence. For five years following release from the juvenile reformatory I remained in the home environment in which my problems had originated. Though the anxiety-ridden family atmosphere had been lessened in severity, it still, nevertheless, had a profound effect upon my behavior and outlook exemplified by my continued failures and shortcomings in educational, vocational, familial, and romantic pursuits and obligations. As soon as I left the house and established an independent living situation, however, I experienced a series of self-discoveries and successes founded on increased competence and confidence. There is no question that this was one of the major turning points in my life.

The ability or opportunity to identify and attain long-range goals and establish a reason for an alternative way of life. Until leaving the home environment, life was merely a series of day-to-day actions and reactions. I was without goals, unable to establish either motive or means to fully conform. Failure and deviance were still a way of life. My only successes were high school graduation and the fact that I had avoided trouble with the law which would have meant reinstitutionalization. Yet during this period and throughout my life, a recurring motif was evident—the theme of learning. Ever since elementary school I had been told that I was capable of learning anything if I just put my mind to it. But I was unable to accept such statements regarding my intellectual abilities and a litany of academic failures reinforced my doubts. I continued to flirt with the educational process, however, aware that there was something about it that intrigued me. When I moved to California and found myself psychologically free to attempt part-time courses in earnest, I discovered both the urge and the capacity to learn. Once begun, the learning process became an all-consuming goal that established a new perception of life. I was able to surmount what had before been my downfall. Conquests and growing confidence and competence followed in other areas of endeavor. I had found a long-range acceptable goal that gave life new meaning.

The devolutionary process was gradual. Just as it had taken years of continual exposure to "unhealthy" circumstances for my delinquent reaction to evolve, it also took an equivalent amount of time to devolve. There was no singular event, no quick cure, no panacea that magically altered my behavior and changed my life, only a series of experiences that contributed, each in its own way, to the eventual outcome. Whatever I was, and whatever I am now, is a direct outgrowth of human dynamics. It was only after the dynamics of my life were altered in a way conducive to promote change that it was possible to seek, find, and master the alternatives.

When I began this book I did not know where it would lead or what I might find. I did, however, have some preconceptions. It seemed to me that the juvenile justice system had made mistakes in the handling of my case. I set out to expose those errors only to find that the good far outweighed the bad, that, in fact, I had been blaming the pain of my youth on those who had been doing their best to help me resolve it.

The juvenile court was the primary recipient of this misplaced blame. I viewed Judge Arkins and Mr. Lantz as villains who had punished my behavior by committing me to institutions. Their involvement seemed oppressive. They knew of my every mistake and indiscretion. I perceived them as self-righteous, punitive, insensitive old men who had excessive power over my life. Through the writing of this book, however, my opinion of these two men has changed. As I began separating emotion from fact, the wisdom of their approach became more apparent, each reading of the records bringing me more in touch with the sincerity of their efforts. I began to understand the importance of the service they had provided, and their dedication to delivering it to the best of their abilities. These officers of the juvenile court had provided the stabilizing force for a child and family in chaos. They were the critical difference that kept us from succumbing to total breakdown.

My opinion of the Pennsylvania Junior Republic has also altered. Both during and after my eighteen-month confinement there, I felt I was being unjustly denied freedom and exposed to a harsh environment. The opportunity to put this institutional experience in perspective has revealed the long-range impact of that placement upon my development. Exposure to a less appropriate setting might have resulted in an entirely different outcome.

However, it is not the purpose of this book to represent the juvenile justice experiences of all delinquents or to suggest that institutionalization is the most appropriate solution for every case. Each child has different needs and should be viewed as a separate entity. What works for the betterment of one may be another's undoing. Nor is it my intention to endorse the actions of all juvenile courts and juvenile justice workers. As in any field of endeavor, some people are better suited than others for such responsibility.

What I originally set out to do in this volume was to display the natural progression of my own delinquency. It was a way for me to put my childhood in perspective while offering insights into the causes of a delinquent response. But as I grew more intimate with the history of my development, I realized that by taking into account the reasons for my abandonment of a delinquent way of life I would be presenting a more complete picture of human growth potential. The fact that I had overcome a disturbed childhood might serve to show that even seriously disturbed delinquents are not necessarily destined to a life of continued crime, deviance, and social dysfunctioning.

In concluding, it is important to give recognition where it is due. The life history herein presented is not atypical. The human organism is marvelously strong, resilient, adaptive, and when provided the right circumstances is capable of overcoming incredible odds. This potential to survive adversity, and even to thrive as a result of it, is one of man's greatest assets. Yet we know less about how people come to conquer hardship than we do about why they are overwhelmed by it. The concept of "recovery" has taken a back seat to the examination of "continued pathology." It is almost as if we have resigned ourselves to failure.

Nowhere is this discrepancy of knowledge—or emphasis—more apparent than in the study of juvenile delinquency. There are mounds of data that explain the nuances of continued delinquency but only scant references to the cessation of past patterns of deviance. When reviewing the literature one is left with the impression that the majority of young people who exhibit pronounced behavioral problems are destined to a lifetime of adjustment difficulties. Institutionalized children would seem beyond hope.

Nothing could be further from the truth. Thousands of young people who have endured experiences as bad or worse than those presented in these pages have abandoned their former delinquent way of life and accomplished a socially-approved adult adjustment. The case histories of "recovery" have, however, gone largely unnoticed and unstudied. As a consequence, we are neglecting insights that might be used to help children currently exhibiting behavioral problems achieve a prosocial behavioral change. It is toward a better understanding of this area—the other side of delinquency—that my own account is directed.